the stories behind every song

ABBA

THANK YOU FOR THE MUSIC

THIS IS A CARLTON BOOK

First published by in Great Britain by Carlton Books Limited 2002
20 Mortimer Street
London W1T 3JW

Text copyright © Robert Scott 2002
Design copyright © Carlton Books Limited 2002

ISBN 1 84222 793 9

Project editor: Lorna Russell
Senior Art Editor: Diane Spender
Design: Michael Spender
Cover design: Karin Fremer
Picture research: Adrian Bentley
Production: Lisa Moore

The publishers would like to thank the following sources for their kind permission
to reproduce the pictures in this book:
Pictorialpress.com: 4, 8-9, 10, 11, 13tl, 16, 17r, 19, 20, 27, 36-37, 39, 45, 56, 57, 91,
110, 122-123, 125, 140, 149bl, 151, 152, 153, 155, 158, 159; /Bäcker: 142, 149tr;
/Hannekroot: 134, 135; /Hussein: 38; /Kohr: 157; /Mayer: 6-7, 12tr, 12bl, 15tr,
17l, 17c, 30, 34, 76-77, 81, 108, 127, 154br; /Van Houten: 85.
Redferns: /Richie Aaron: 138; /Fin Costello: 22; /Glenn A. Baker Archive: 116;
/Michael Ochs Archives: 25, 73, 156; /Keith Morris: 84, 114, 146-147;
/Petra Niemeier: 86, 87; /Mike Prior: 23; /RB: 71, 92, 117, 132;
/David Redfern: 42, 100; /Gai Terrell: 15bl, 154tr.
Retna Ltd: 104, 115, 144; /Adrian Boot: 66, 94, 95; /Imperial Press: 13br;
/King Collection: 70, 143, 150; /Neal Preston: 89; /Michael Putland: 44, 68;
/Sunshine/G. de Roos: 107, 145; /Sunshine/G. Hanekroot: 79.
Rex Features: 1, 3, 14, 52, 55, 61, 63, 120, 128, 130-131, 148; /Dezo Hoffmann: 51;
/Media Press: 46-47, 112; /David Thorpe: 98; /Richard Young: 101.

Every effort has been made to acknowledge correctly and contact the source
and/or copyright holder of each picture, and Carlton Publishing Group apologises for any
unintentional errors or omissions which will be corrected in future editions of this book.

Printed and bound in Dubai

CARLTON
BOOKS

ROBERT SCOTT

the stories behind every song

ABBA

THANK YOU FOR THE MUSIC

CONTENTS

FOREWORD

WHO COULD HAVE PREDICTED, when four Swedes cobbled their initials together in the early Seventies, that their new clumsy, childlike name was to become a household word, shorthand for pop at its very finest? ABBA – Benny Andersson (keyboards/ vocals), Bjorn Ulvaeus (guitar/vocals) and vocalists Agnetha Faltskog (the blonde) and Anni-Frid Lyngstad (the redhead) – won the Eurovision Song Contest with "Waterloo", which was their second attempt, and unlike most Eurovision overnight sensations, they never looked back.

Although the American market was, for a while, to retain reservations, the rest of the planet's record-buyers capitulated immediately.

Euphoric hits like "Dancing Queen", "Mamma Mia" and "Take A Chance On Me" and melancholy marvels such as "The Winner Takes It All" and "Knowing Me, Knowing You" are to this day difficult to dislike and impossible to avoid.

The flamboyant foursome's interesting fashion decisions meant their image was indelibly etched across the Seventies (an era which is increasingly presenting a case for itself as pop's true, if tacky, golden age) and the complex personal relationships within the group inspired many of their later, more forlorn and mature lyrics. Eager, sometimes crass, but bizarrely talented, Abba split in the early Eighties, leaving a musical legacy that's been often mimicked but never matched.

So what is it about this camp yet cunning body of work that makes it so memorable, so adored to this day? We'll try to find out. When we celebrate the songs of Abba, we celebrate pop…

ABBA

INTRODUCTION

ALTHOUGH THE STORY ON RECORD BEGAN with 1973's *Ring Ring* album, Benny and Bjorn had first met as early as 1966. Bjorn was then a member of American-influenced, extremely uncool but locally successful folk group The Hootenanny Singers (formerly The West Bay Singers), while Benny was honing his craft as the fulcrum of The Hep Stars. The first hit song he wrote for them, "Sunny Girl", topped the Swedish charts for weeks. The two young Swedish pop idols, who clearly already had their fair quota of shared experiences, became friends.

Inevitably, in time, they took to composing songs together. Publisher Stig Anderson, head of the Hootenannys' record label Polar and of course soon to be a major figure in Abba's career, had a dream. Which was to be Svengali to a Swedish pop combo that could cross over to an international public.

Two female solo stars were simultaneously in the ascendant. Anni-Frid, known to most as Frida, and Agnetha, were dance band vocalists getting a foothold in the pop chart hills. Benny and Frida fell for each other, and were engaged by the spring of

1970. Bjorn and Agnetha, a fiery, explosive couple did likewise, marrying the next year. Collaborations ensued, with the girls' first backing vocals for their chaps appearing on the Swedish hit "Hej Gamle Man!" ("Hey Old Man!"). The quartet of lovebirds experimented by treading the boards in Gothenburg as a cabaret act: Festfolk (Party People, or Engaged Couples). They bombed.

However, the Benny and Bjorn songwriting team was enjoying some success, and penning hits for a stream of Swedish acts. Benny was doing well as solo artist too, oddly enough as a purveyor of some radical cover versions. But as a duo, the first significant breakthrough came with "She's My Kind Of Girl", which, inexplicably to anyone concerned, sold half a million copies in Japan. (It had originally been written for a slightly suspect movie that had emerged under that shiftiest of titles, *The Seduction Of Inga*). Other singles followed, with the girls not credited on backing vocals. There was even a 1970 album, *Lycka ("Happiness"). Things were about to get happier.*

Stig had remained reluctant to allow the girls equal billing. He wanted Bjorn and Benny's predominantly female fan club to be allowed the

illusion that their pin-ups were "available". And even a businessman like Stig considered the notion of a loved-up, snuggly foursome to be a tad too cosy and kitsch for the broader reaches of global pop. Not very wild and decadent, was it?

"THE FOUR PERFORMED IN TOKYO, WHERE THE SUCCESS OF *SHE'S MY KIND OF GIRL* MEANT THEY WERE RECEIVED RAPTUROUSLY."

Yet Bjorn's enthusiasm, and the sorting-out of some tricky contractual issues, allowed destiny to override realism. The four performed in Tokyo, where the success of "She's My Kind Of Girl" meant they were received rapturously. They had a taste of being treated as pop royalty. Confidence rebuilt, they recorded further material with the girls front-stage centre, and insisted to Stig that this was the way forward. There were arguments. Stig gave in, thinking the couples perhaps just needed to get this out of their system, and that when it all went pear-shaped he could pick up the reins again and guide the guys to stardom his way, according to his own masterplan. "People Need Love" was

released, attributed to Bjorn, Benny, Agnetha & Frida, and with the girls' close harmonies wowing listeners, was a smash hit across Scandinavia.

It didn't do it for the rest of the world, though, despite coming out on Hugh Hefner's Playboy label in America. There, it reached number 115. Still, Stig was sort of onside, the girls were in, and further singles emerged under the unwieldy, four-barrelled moniker. Eurovision beckoned. They knew it was naff, but they also knew it meant a massive T.V. audience of around fifty million.

The guys, pressurised by Stig to conjure up an instant winner, carved out the Spector-influenced "Ring, Ring". Legendary songwriter Neil Sedaka and his colleague Phil Cody drafted English lyrics. Agnetha took lead vocals. She sang, pregnant, at the Stockholm heats. Heats which a cocky Abba, bafflingly, did not win. They came third. They were, to put it mildly, stunned. There was anger. There were tears. Maybe the idea of the four of them together didn't work after all.

Or maybe it did, and the judges didn't know their knees from their elbows. The Swedish and English versions of "Ring, Ring" were released as two singles. They immediately took up residency at number one and number two on the Swedish charts. Abba decided to stay together. And make an album. Of course they'd never entertain the notion of competing in that stupid, sad Eurovision Song Contest thing again. Would they?

Right now, it was time for that first album to chime out…

The (F)Abba Four

Before we answer its call, however, perhaps we need to ascertain a little more about these four so-normal-and-yet-somehow-so-very-weird musicians. Contrary to what most of us who grew up during the Seventies might believe, they did not arrive fully-formed in a puff of billowing, magical smoke. They'd had childhoods, careers, elations and disappointments, even prior to the Abba arc. A little background on each of the four characters might help us to colour in the picture. How were these stars born?

Agnetha

Alphabetical order, then. Agnetha. The one you noticed first and remembered longest, and particularly if you were male. The bubbly singer who everyone fondly imagined must be vulnerable beneath that sex-symbol veneer, but by all accounts was a firebrand, engaging in frequent

heated rows with Bjorn, and was in later years a victim of depression and a virtual recluse. The one who, to her eventual distress, always gleaned more reviews of her bottom (yes, there was a "sexiest backside in pop" even before the age of Kylie) and her hair than of her vocals. So how did the pop phenonomenon known as Agnetha come to pass?

Agnetha Ase Faltskog was born in April 1950, in Jonkoping, a lakeside town in the south of Sweden. Her father, a keen pivot of the local amateur dramatics society, introduced her to the stage. Ingvar would often put on shows in his spare time. These would feature songs and sketches he'd written himself. Agnetha made her stage debut at the tender age of six, at a Christmas show Ingvar had set up for senior citizens. Legend has it that as Agnetha recited something called "Billy Boy", her pants fell down, to hoots of geriatic

laughter. There is no subsequent record of Agnetha ever reciting "Billy Boy", or dropping her pants, while onstage with Abba.

Bouncing back from this trial, she learned piano, composing ditties inspired by the tales of the Scandinavian trolls. Every Sunday, she'd play the harpsichord at church. By thirteen, she'd begun singing and performing with two friends, locally and in the neighbouring area of Smaland. She left school at fifteen, deciding against further education, and took a job as a telephonist at a car sales company. You could, of course, argue that this experience informed and fuelled her vocal interpretation of "Ring, Ring", though that would be a bit silly and overzealous of you. One thing Agnetha did learn here was that a local dance band needed a female vocalist, weekends only. She applied to its leader, one Berngt Enghardt, who gave her the spot.

The band did well. Weekday gigs were offered: a problem for Agnetha. Should she pack in her day job? She did. The family weren't best pleased. Soon she'd split up with her boyfriend another Bjorn, consigned, I'm afraid, to history's oblivion bin, and written a song about the break-up. "Jag Var Sa Kar" ("I Was So In Love"), possibly just a little bit autobiographical, became a firm favourite with fans of the Berngt Enghardt Band. Berngt sent a demo tape to former Swedish rock star and now A&R scout and producer Little Gerhard. He liked two things about Berngt's band Agnetha's voice and Agnetha's song. And when he saw what she looked like, well, that certainly didn't do any harm.

At first, when he rang, she thought it was a hoax. Invited to Stockholm to record her song, she started believing. If your pants have fallen down on your first public performance, it's understandable if you're a touch sceptical about things. First though, she had to break it to Berndt that she was required and the band weren't. "It was a tough situation for me", she later recalled.

In 1967, accompanied by her father, she took the train to Stockholm. Nervously she entered the impressive Philips Recording Studio. It was "the most exciting moment of my life. My heart was in my mouth...I was walking on air and floated into the room as if I were on a cloud", she says in Paul Snaith's *Abba: The Music Still Goes On*. She recorded four songs, including another of her own, "Utan Dig" ("Without You"). By January 1968, "Jag Var Sa Kar" went straight into the national top three. The media loved her, and Agnetha, aged seventeen, was immediately famous. She signed a deal with CBS/Cupol Records.

Living alone in Stockholm, she wrote and recorded several more solo hits, usually concerning on broken hearts. Her self-titled debut album spent weeks on the charts. After a farewell tour with Berngt and the boys, she undertook a solo tour of Sweden's "folk parks". Somehow, in the midst of all this success, she managed to enlist at stage school, and visit schools in her hometown area to promote the value of dental hygiene. Though the fact tends to get overshadowed by the runaway Abba story, she was already one of Sweden's biggest female celebrities.

Also during 1968, Agnetha got engaged to a German producer and songwriter, Dieter Zimmerman. She was nibbling at the German charts, and Dieter vowed to help her career there. But once there, she loathed the material German producers were urging on her. That angle, and the relationship with Zimmerman, rapidly petered out. In Sweden, though, the hits kept coming. In the summer of '69, she was recording a T.V. programme when she met one Bjorn Ulvaeus...

Anni-Frid, or "Frida"

Strict adherence to alphabetical order insists that the camera now pans to Anni-Frid "Frida" Lyngstad, who seems to have attracted controversy even before her birth in Norway in November 1945. Her mother Synni, just nineteen, fell for a German soldier, Alfred Haase, posted to the Narvik suburb of Bjorkasen during the Second World War. Even as the war drew to a close, Synni was less than popular with the local people, who remembered only too keenly the recent, German occupation of Norway. Synni's friends deserted her, and she was even spat at in the street.

When Alfred was ordered back to Germany, he promised he'd return and marry the now-pregnant Synni. When her daughter was born, Synni named her Anni-Frid, after her own grandmother. Her German soldier never did come back, and tragically Anni-Frid's mother died aged only twenty-one. Synni's mother had to care for and raise the baby that neighbours referred to disparagingly as "the German child". Sensibly enough, she realised a fresh start was necessary, and moved to Sweden. After a couple of years they settled in Eskillstuna, around a hundred miles from Stockholm. Here, nights were dark, cold and long. Anni-Frid's grandmother encouraged her to sing folk songs – of both Swedish and Norwegian origin – beside the fireplace. By the age of ten, Anni-Frid was performing in concerts and Red Cross parties at the local village hall. By thirteen, she had turned professional – she had to lie about her age – with a restaurant's dance band. Everyone said she sang, and looked, mature for her age.

After further experience with jazz bands, Anni-Frid formed her own combo The Anni-Frid Four. Locally, they did fine. Anni-Frid lived with, then had a baby with, then married, her bass player, Ragnar Fredriksson. Their child Hans was born in 1963; they married the next year. Yet the couple had a sense that they could take their music to wider audiences. Anni-Frid's grandmother was again left capably holding the baby, while Anni-Frid, who'd been taking singing lessons with acclaimed opera singer Folke Andersson, and Ragnar toured. A sec

second child, Lieselotte, was born in 1967, but Anni-Frid's musical ambition were growing nonetheless.

To her surprise, she won a national talent contest in Stockholm, and was instantly offered a record deal by EMI. Her ballad "En Ledig Dag" ("A Day Off") didn't take the charts by storm, but her self-titled debut album won glowing reviews, with one national newspaper claiming, "Anni-Frid is one of our best singers, vocally, technically, and musically." She felt she had to move to Stockholm to capitalise. She separated from Ragnar amicably, leaving the two children with him in Eskillstuna.

Making her base in a small Stockholm flat, she toured the popular "folk parks" with Lasse Berghagen, then for two years worked nightclubs with Charlie Norman. Her career was now building gradually rather than spectacularly, with her records regularly appearing in the charts. She made plentiful television appearances. On tour in Malmo, in early 1969, she was playing a nightclub next door to one where The Hep Stars were performing. She only met Benny Andersson briefly, but a few weeks later the pair recognised each other when serving as panellists on a midnight radio show. They got along rather well. By August, they were engaged.

Benny

Benny Andersson had been born in the Stockholm suburb of Vallinby to a music-loving family in December 1946. His parents – Costa and Efraim – had confirmed obsolete comic British stereotypes of hurdy-gurdy Swedes by spending their evenings playing folk tunes on the accordion. Music ran in the family's blood. Benny had his first accordion as a small child, and at ten was playing the piano. He left school at fifteen to focus fully on music. Through the early Sixties he performed live at youth clubs, often with singer Christina Gronwall. Soon Christina was his fiancée, and the couple had a son, Peter, as early as 1963. Benny supported his family by working as a janitor for his father's firm, and played keyboards with a local band, Elverlerts Spelmanslag.

This outfit buddied up with a rising local group, the Hep Stars, who wasted little time in poaching Benny as their new keyboardist. In early '65 the gloriously named Hep Stars performed their first record, "Cadillac", on TV, and within a few weeks sensationally occupied three of the top four places on the Swedish pop charts. Benny enthusiastically began contributing to writing duties, and the band recorded his composition "No Response". Also in 1965, he and Christina had a daughter, Helene, but separated shortly afterwards. Benny cheered up, no doubt, when the Hep Stars' first Andersson-penned hit, "Sunny Girl", became a huge number one. Other hits such as "It's Nice To Be Back", "Wedding" and "Consolation" offered further, er, consolation. The Hep Stars were now the country's biggest band. They'd won gold discs with their first three albums and five singles.

"BENNY HAD HIS FIRST ACCORDION AS A SMALL CHILD, AND AT TEN WAS PLAYING THE PIANO. HE LEFT SCHOOL AT FIFTEEN TO FOCUS FULLY ON MUSIC."

But in an echo of a tale we hear so often in pop music, the naïve, excited, overworked young stars were financially well and truly ripped off. Shady business deals and an abortive, ill-conceived film project left the Hep Stars with mounting debts. Even years later, Benny faced a monstrous tax bill, which ate alarmingly big chunks of his future Abba earnings. At one stage he was forced to send all the royalties from his songs direct to the Inland Revenue.

Disillusioned, the Hep Stars split in 1969. A few members kept the name, while Benny teamed up with the singer Lotte Walker, formerly with American band The Sherrys. But he didn't lose contact with one Bjorn Ulvaeus, his friend from the Hootenanny Singers. In an all-night session in summer '69, they co-wrote their first song, "Isn't It Easy?" Within the same few weeks, Bjorn met Agnetha. Easy, no, but something special was beginning to come together…

Bjorn

Bjorn Kristian Ulvaeus was born in April 1945 in Gothenburg, though six years later his family moved to Vastervik on the east coast. His parents loved music, and bought him his first guitar at an early age. Oddly, Bjorn developed a youthful passion for skiffle. The unlikely Lonnie Donegan-lover was snapped up as a precocious teen by folk band the West Bay Singers. They had patterned cardigans and wispy beards, but we'll try not to hold that against them too vehemently. They toured Europe in a Volvo, which was all very exciting for the impressionable young Bjorn.

Back in Sweden, Bjorn's mother, Aina, entered them for a national talent contest. Unlike Anni-Frid, they did not win. Good did come of the experience, however – a talent scout, Bengt Bernhag, noticed them. And he had a partner with whom he'd just formed a record company, Polar Music. And this partner's name was Stikkan Andersson – "Stig" for short. He was to become the most important player, outside the four principals, in the Abba story.

"BJORN ULVAEUS WAS INCREASINGLY ENJOYING WORKING WITH BENNY ANDERSSON, WRITING AND PRODUCING..."

The West Bays recorded a demo for Polar, and after a formal audition were signed as the new label's first act. Stig and Bengt suggested the band sing in Swedish rather than English, and that they change their name. Hard though it is to imagine a businessman suggesting a band change their name to The Hootenanny Singers as opposed to anything but The Hootenanny Singers, this was the unorthodox Stig's will. The newly named group got television exposure, winning their next talent show, and a debut hit with "Jag Vantar Vid Min Mila". They were at the time the only group in the charts singing in the native tongue. Bjorn celebrated by passing his exams and graduating!

The Hootenannys worked the "folk park" circuit for two years, simultaneously writing, recording and promoting. They toured Germany, and tested the waters in England and America by releasing a single, "No Time", under the pseudonym of Northern Lights. It flopped. In '66 Bjorn and his colleagues had to serve eighteen months of National Service. Somehow, they, or Stig, wangled enough regular leave to keep the band actively performing. The hits kept on coming, and in '67 their Swedish-language interpretation of the well-known Tom Jones classic, "The Green, Green Grass Of Home" "En Sand En Gand For Langesen" was their best seller yet.

With National Service completed, all four of the Hootenanny Singers opted to take on further courses of study. Bjorn went to Stockholm University, where he studied business, law and economics. In the early days, his education often came to the aid of Polar Music. His self-written solo material was beginning to emerge on B-sides, and it was no surprise to those close to him and to the Polar people when he bagged a few hits himself. "Baby, Those Are The Rules", "Froken Fredriksson" and "Raring" (a cover of Bobby Goldsboro's wonderfully sentimental weepie "Honey") established him as a burgeoning solo artist. The Hootenannys disbanded. Bjorn Ulvaeus was increasingly enjoying working with Benny Andersson, writing and producing for others. They masterminded several hits. Performing his own latest smash on TV in Stockholm, Bjorn met, and was instantly attracted to, young singer Agnetha Faltskog...

Come Together...

All of which youthful success, romance and optimism just about brings us to the tail end

"A NEW ERA WAS SOON TO DAWN, AND OUR CAST

OF FOUR WERE TO PROVE, COLLECTIVELY, TO BE ONE

OF ITS LEADING LIGHTS."

of the Sixties. A new era was soon to dawn, and our cast of four were to prove, collectively, to be one of its leading lights. Benny and Bjorn were by now great pals and constant co-writers. By late '69 Benny and Anni-Frid were living together in Stockholm, and Bjorn and Agnetha were dating. As the Sixties mutated into the Seventies, the girls were pursuing their solo careers, while the boys were busy providing others with hits. Agnetha's third album *Sam Jar Ag* (On My Own) was another smash. Everything was going rather well, as long as you don't object to the boys scoring *The Seduction Of Inga* – a very Swedish kind of movie, to err on the euphemistic side.

On a happy-couples foursome holiday to Cyprus in April 1970, Bjorn and Agnetha announced their engagement. Refreshed, back in Sweden, Bjorn and Benny began their first self-produced album as a pair. *Lycka* (Happiness) featured eleven songs, including the already-mentioned "Hej Gamle Man", the first song to include all four Abba members together. The Festfolk Quartet's live experiment came and, perhaps mercifully, went (although some kind reviews could be pointed to). The international market Stig craved began to vaguely notice Bjorn and Benny's potential, and Anni-Frid started a noble tradition by entering the 1971 Swedish Eurovision heats and losing comprehensively. Her second solo opus, *Frida*, which was produced by Benny, did rather better.

Arguably, though, it was Agnetha's year. She took the starring role of Mary Magdalene in the Gothenburg production of *Jesus Christ Superstar*, the famous Andrew Lloyd Webber and Tim Rice musical, opening to ecstatic reviews. "I Don't Know How To Love Him" gave her another huge spin-off hit. Bjorn proposed, and the celebrity couple – the 1971 Swedish version of Posh'n'Becks, perhaps – married in the village church at Verum in July. Several thousand fans and well-wishers crammed into the small village for the showbiz wedding of the year. Benny – who else? – played Mendelsohn's Wedding March on the church organ, thus fulfilling a lifelong ambition. He also played his own composition, the Hep Stars' hit "Wedding", presumably with the happy couple's permission. Bjorn and Agnetha then left the church, through a hectic crush of photographers, in a horse-drawn carriage.

The following morning, however, the celebrations were muted when tragic news broke. With awful timing, Bengt Bernhag, Stig Andersson's best friend and business partner, had committed suicide. When everyone had assimilated the explosion of events a few days later, Stig asked the usefully educated Bjorn if he'd take over Bengt's position at Polar. Bjorn suggested he shared the role with Benny.

By mid-autumn, Bjorn and Benny were officially Polar's in-house producers. Their first work? A Hootenanny Singers album. Various other writing and production work continued apace, and in 1972 there was no longer any conceivable reason for the pair not to release an album themselves. Contrary to Stig's initial instincts, they were both determined that Agnetha and Anni-Frid would grace all the songs with their voices. People heard the stuff. And lo, the stuff was good. Though there were still a few twists and turns in store, *Ring Ring* – the first album by Abba – was now just a dial tone away…

RING RING 1973

Recorded March 1972 - March 1973 at Metronome, Europafilm, and KMH Studios, Stockholm.

Produced by Benny Andersson and Bjorn Ulvaeus. Engineered by Michael B. Tretow.

Musicians: Bjorn Ulvaeus (acoustic guitar), Janne Schaffer (acoustic and electric guitar), Benny Andersson (piano, mellotron), Rutgar Gunnarsson (bass), Mike Watson (bass), Ola Brunkert (drums), Roger Palm (drums), Sven-Olof Walldoff (string arrangements on "I Am Just A Girl").

Vocals by Bjorn, Benny, Agnetha and Frida.

RING, RING

ANOTHER TOWN, ANOTHER TRAIN

DISILLUSION

PEOPLE NEED LOVE

I SAW IT IN THE MIRROR

NINA, PRETTY BALLERINA

LOVE ISN'T EASY (BUT IT SURE IS HARD ENOUGH)

ME AND BOBBY AND BOBBY'S BROTHER

HE IS YOUR BROTHER

SHE'S MY KIND OF GIRL

I AM JUST A GIRL

ROCK'N'ROLL BAND

Bonus tracks on 2001 Reissue:

MERRY-GO-ROUND

SANTA ROSA

RING, RING (SWEDISH VERSION)

RING RING IS AN ALBUM MADE BY A BAND THAT DIDN'T KNOW IF IT EXISTED OR NOT. IF INITIALLY A WARM RESPONSE IN SWEDEN AND JAPAN TO SINGLES LIKE "PEOPLE NEED LOVE" AND "SANTA ROSA" PERSUADED STIG ANDERSSON THAT BJORN AND BENNY WERE WORKING ALONG THE RIGHT LINES BY MERGING MUSICALLY WITH THEIR OTHER HALVES, RING RING WAS – BIZARRELY – AN ALBUM PRECIPITATED BY A PERCEIVED FAILURE.

The first Eurovision debacle and the snubbing of the title song had ruffled the quartet's pride, riling these avowed perfectionists. Only two of the eleven judges had given the song any points at all. (Interesting trivia: one of these, singer Peter Holm, was a decade later to marry and divorce UK actress Joan Collins).

Yet the song went on to become such a hit in their homeland that an accompanying album was deemed essential. Stig had to swallow his doubts and allow Abba to be born. Abba weren't sure if they were Abba. Or for how long. But the two couples definitely wanted to get their songs out there…

Little did anyone realise what a pop monster was about to be launched.

When "Ring, Ring" failed to pull the bells of the Eurovision judges, in February 1973 – it lost to somebody called Malta Duo – Agnetha consoled herself by, thirteen days later, giving birth to a baby girl, Linda.

Linda gave her first press conference at the Stockholm hospital, aged two days. The two versions of "Ring, Ring" – Swedish and English –– took up the top two places in the national charts. There were still issues to be resolved vis-à-vis the girls' solo recording contracts, but Bjorn, Benny and Stig decided that the four should release an album, almost as a hobby, to see what happened.

It was finally waved off into the world in March '73, with Anni-Frid officially being referred to as Frida. A bit of a mix-and-match of a record, it included all the group's singles to date, plus a hodgepodge of other, cobbled-together material. Some had been written years earlier for other acts. Some consisted of revamped versions of songs previously recorded in Swedish. There were remixes, overdubs and resurrected B-sides. Nevertheless, it was a chart-topping album in Belgium and a big success in Holland, Norway and South Africa. It spawned various hit singles all over the place. What it *didn't* do was make an impact in the crucial commercial areas – the United States, the U.K, or Japan. (Later, when Abba were a household name, it sold rather better).

"IT CATCHES THE SPIRIT OF THE ERA'S LESS CHIC POP STYLINGS AS WELL AS ANYTHING ELSE."

As a listening experience, *Ring Ring* has a jolly, if patchy, feel. It's very evident that Bjorn and Benny were seeking to emulate American and British sounds they'd heard: it catches the spirit of the era's less chic pop stylings as well as anything else – lots of booming oompah-oompah choruses and peace-and-love platitudes. They want to be what at the time passed for hip, but haven't yet quite thrown off their folkie-roots shackles. Some tracks are breezy, others leaden. The most important thing for Abba here was that they were stretching, reaching out – if they don't quite find the magic Abba formula at this point (in fact, they miss it with a comic pratfall once or twice), it's a vital bridge. In flashes, you can discern it coming together, "it" being the unique splendour of the Abba sound. They're not there yet, but they are clearly growing into the new shapes they're creating, heading in the right direction…

Ring, Ring

The single "Ring, Ring" sounds more 1973 now than it did during 1973. To explain: everything about it now evokes the era. It didn't seem very *zeitgesty* then, but a cursory glance at the British singles charts of the time tells you there was definitely an early Seventies pop "sound". "Ring, Ring" is just one of a million throwaway three-minute gems from the period that are catchy, for-gettable, hedonistic, brilliant in their way. The UK glam rock movement was beginning to blow away the cobwebs of bearded, tie-dyed progressive rock, and the pop charts were feeling like some harmless, bubbly, fizzy fun again.

If T.Rex's chart dominance was waning, their influence remained, with David Bowie picking up the baton. Nicky Chinn and Mike Chapman were a hugely successful production/writing team who churned out hot hits for the likes of Mud, The Sweet and Suzi Quatro. Donny Osmond and David Cassidy adorned every teenage girl's bedroom wall, while other pre-eminent names included Rod Stewart, Gary Glitter, Elton John, Slade and Wizzard. And there was still a place for cuddly-couples pop ballads, as Dawn and The New Seekers demonstrated.

If 1972's best-selling single in the U.K. – "Amazing Grace" by the Royal Scots Dragoon Guards Band -– was a red herring, 1973's end-of-year listings were more representative of the crazy sounds the kids were listening to. Top singles of

this year included Dawn's "Tie A Yellow Ribbon", The Sweet's "Blockbuster" and Slade's "Cum On Feel The Noize", while the top twenty best-selling albums of ''73 featured no less than four from the epoch-defining, stardust-sprinkling Bowie.

It seemed you could win by being as weird as *A Clockwork Orange* (the soundtrack to Stanley Kubrick's controversial film was a huge seller) or Alice Cooper, or as homely as Peters & Lee or Gilbert O'Sullivan. No wonder Abba – colourful but wholesome – at first fell between several stools.

The looping guitar motif, simple but effective chords and chirpy rhythms of "Ring, Ring" are very much of their time. The girls' vocals rise higher than Pinky and Perky, as if gorged on helium, and the phrase "happiest sound of them all" is indisputably onomatopoeic. There are tricky hooks galore, the drums try too hard to emphasise anything they can emphasise, and the chorus digs into your brain. It's three minutes of perfect pop, achieving precisely what it sets out to achieve – perhaps too precisely. It was a typical Bjorn/Benny melody, but they'd had a helping hand with the words.

Neil Sedaka, an idol of Agnetha's, was no stranger to the perfect three-minute pop song. From the late Fifties onwards, as part of the legendary Brill Building hit factory set-up, he'd penned disposable classics aplenty, such as "Oh Carol", "Calendar Girl", "Stupid Cupid" and "Happy Birthday Sweet Sixteen", singing many himself. His stock was high at this time. Stig Andersson knew Sedaka through his contacts in the publishing side of the music business, and approached him to come up with English lyrics for "Ring, Ring". (The title had been Stig's own). Sedaka loved the track and, after a few days' work with his then-partner Phil Cody, delivered. If there's nothing particularly original about a pop lyric wherein a lover waits all alone by the phone for the object of their desire to call, such a cliché has rarely been honed as concisely and astutely as this. At last Stig could scent that elusive international breakthrough hit.

For all Stig's worldwide music biz networking, Abba's flop in the Swedish heats of Eurovision was still a massive blow. He'd had a terrific reaction to the track originally, but now people began to back off and hedge their bets. The image of Agnetha singing in a green maternity smock also hadn't helped to fuel any potential investors' fantasies.

Any such doubts were forgotten when "Ring, Ring" sold like the proverbial hot cakes. Within a year of release, it had, worldwide, passed the half-million mark. In the U.K. it passed relatively unnoticed, however. Epic Records put it out in October '73, after half a dozen other companies had turned it down. Stig's chum Paul Atkinson, once a guitarist with The Zombies (Sixties hitmakers with "She's Not There") was the only man who believed. Abba signed to Epic for a modest sum, but a decent royalty rate. Epic weren't too troubled: "Ring, Ring" sold around five thousand copies in Britain, not disturbing the charts.

For their part, Abba were too busy dealing with their success almost everywhere else to worry unduly about this setback. The album was doing just fine. The actual sound of the single "Ring, Ring", however, with its Phil Spector-ish resonances and vocal overlaying (initiated by Bjorn and Benny's new wunderkind engineer, Michael Tretow) was an indication of where Abba might aspire to go next…

Another Town, Another Train

Another Bjorn and Benny composition, which verges on the twee despite its theme of restless wanderlust. Its narrator must leave (bed, presumably) as "day is dawning". Although "you and I had a groovy time", he just has "to move along". You get the sense they'd like this melodic ballad to resemble Simon and Garfunkel: in truth, it's so wholesome it's closer to The Bachelors. Wild and decadent it isn't. Woolly cardigans it is. He's a drifter, this chap, "a no-good bum" apparently, who'll spend his life in railway stations. He's unconvincing.

After a mawkish flutey intro, the guys' vocals are unimaginative and the girls' fleeting entrance is as close as the song gets to kicking into life. Benny's piano-playing's pretty when it should be more wanton. At best, you could call this a dry run for "Fernando" – certainly there are hints here of motifs which were better utilised on that anthem. But "Another Town, Another Train" is a give-away that the album began as a Bjorn & Benny album with Agnetha and Frida in guest roles. The formula wasn't firmed up yet.

> **" *RING, RING* SOLD AROUND FIVE THOUSAND COPIES IN BRITAIN. "**

Disillusion

In which, for the first and last time, Agnetha was to contribute writing duties to a group album. Not that it was a stinker. This is an overblown torch ballad (co-written with Bjorn), which, ironically, suffers from under-production. Her stagey vocal reminds us that her head was probably in a very *Jesus Christ Superstar* place: she sounds trained. It's the kind of song you can imagine Rice & Lloyd-Webber creating for an Elaine Paige or Barbara Dickson. Agnetha's note-perfect, but paper-thin; there's no blood and guts to her polished performance, no raw emotion, although she wakes up a little in the second verse. And if she looked the part of an ice queen, Agnetha wasn't one… she just does a fair impression of one here, and it's inappropriate. But let's not be too harsh, huh? She *had* just had a baby.

The chaps' production is smooth, pleasant, uninspired. There's a cuteness to the way Agnetha pronounces "reason" as "ree-ssonn". She clearly held a fondness for the song, as she later recorded a richer, Swedish version for a solo album.

She was to express pride that Bjorn and Benny had wanted the track on the album, as she held their songwriting talents in such awe. Prone to insecurity, she probably didn't believe, at this stage, that it was strong enough, and her doubt seeps through the lyrics, which sigh of worlds breaking down as she wishes, and hopes, and chases shadows. The sad thing is that, for all its flaws, it's far from being one of the album's weakest cuts. In any lesser group, Agnetha would have been given more opportunities to nurture her writing abilities. Once the Abba hit machine was rolling though, nobody was going to take too many risks or attempt to fix a team strategy that wasn't broke…

People Need Love

There are few hit songs of which you can confidently declare, "This was patently influenced by the short-lived early Seventies hit-makers Blue Mink". This, however, is one such song. Benny made no secret of the fact that he'd listened to this outfit, as well as equally transient chart-toppers Middle Of The Road ("Chirpy Chirpy Cheep Cheep"), and tried to emulate their simple, nursery-rhyme melodies. British "band" Blue Mink, a shifting collective of session musicians, would trade vocals between nominal front-persons Madeline Bell and Roger Cook. What Benny liked was the way male and female vocals would interact, take turns, bounce off each other. Blue Mink, whose hits included "Melting Pot" and "Banner Man", would often sing about racial harmony and loving your brother/sister/neighbour, but instead of brow-beating the listener, would woo them with irresistible, cheesy choruses and rhythms as subtle as a sledgehammer. That, thought, Benny, works for me.

> **"WHAT BENNY LIKED WAS THE WAY MALE AND FEMALE VOCALS WOULD INTERACT, TAKE TURNS, BOUNCE OFF EACH OTHER."**

So the lyrics here are all about "trust from a fellow man", and aren't shy of stuff like "flowers in a desert need a drop of rain". There may be something a bit suspect about the gender roles implied – try deconstructing this, Germaine: "Man has always wanted a woman by his side, to keep him company/Women always knew that it takes a man to get matrimonial harmony". In fact, "matrimonial" is possibly the worst word you could try to cram into a pop song anyway, but then this is Bjorn &

Agnetha & Benny & Frida we're talking about, the fluffy foursome in excelsis... at least at this stage...

Massed harmonies, a stonkingly big and cumbersome chorus, a plodding paean to family values. Phew, rock'n'roll! The inevitable "la la la" refrain sounds very Cliff Richard, and the bass player is obviously wearing cement boots. On his hands. There's even some sub-Frank Ifield yodelling from the girls, over the fade-out... shameless, shameless, although it at least distracts from the boys' nasal mutterings. Completely bonkers, then, and very early Seventies.

And, of course, it worked. When it came to Bjorn and Benny's nose for a hit, "Ring, Ring" was the exception which proved the rule. "People Need Love" – thanks to the girls' minor vocal contributions often referred to as the first Abba song – had already been a Swedish hit when released in April '72 by "Bjorn, Benny, Agnetha and Anni-Frid". The session from which it was spawned was debatably the first Abba recording session. But even Hugh Hefner's approval couldn't make it a hit in America...

I Saw It In The Mirror

Recorded hastily as a filler, along with two other tracks, less than a fortnight before the album's release, this dirge had first been conceived as a 1970 b-side for Billy G-Son. Which doesn't show as much as it might. Though it'd love to have a soulful feel (and Billy G-Son had given it one), "I Saw It In The Mirror" is dragged back by a plodding, sleepy rhythm section. Bjorn and Benny are no Al Green – in fact, their reedy voices together bear echoes of Speedy Keen, the man who sang

Thunderclap Newman's neo-psychedelic Sixties anthem "Something In The Air". Yet, as the narrator tells us that he sees his own sadness when he looks in the mirror, something great happens. The girls come in on a call-and-response of "this boy cries", and it's wonderful. Suddenly what Abba could yet achieve becomes perfectly clear. Once they work out how to fully exploit the interplay between the male and female voices, they're going to be something special. The female voices ensure the song climaxes on a high, too. There's a glimpse of the still-brewing magic here...

All of which doesn't alter the fact that, in polls taken among the long-term Abba fan base, "I Saw It In The Mirror" has on occasion been voted the least popular Abba song ever. Which is quite an achievement, in its way. But then, who can say whether such polls are the fairest of them all?

"ONCE THEY WORK OUT HOW TO FULLY EXPLOIT THE INTERPLAY BETWEEN THE MALE AND FEMALE VOICES, THEY'RE GOING TO BE SOMETHING SPECIAL."

Nina, Pretty Ballerina

This is a plinky-plonk, irritating stream of Euro-pop tropes, redeemed only by a degree of camp and the thought that it may have proven to be a rough blueprint for the majestic "Dancing Queen". "Nina, Pretty Ballerina", as jaunty as the day is long, fails to charm in every place where "Dancing Queen" succeeds, but could be taken, like the album as a whole, as a necessary step towards pinning down that magic formula.

> " *NINA, PRETTY BALLERINA*, AS JAUNTY AS THE DAY IS LONG, FAILS TO CHARM IN EVERY PLACE WHERE *DANCING QUEEN* SUCCEEDS. "

Guitar licks intrude showily, like belches. Canned applause rather tastelessly breaks out. Again, the gender issues are dodgy – Nina's "just another woman with no name" (so her name isn't, like, Nina, then?) who turns out to be "the queen of the dancing floor" (remind you of anything?) every Friday night.

She's "shy", "uncertain", and "just like Cinderella". Soon, Abba would go the ball, and earn real applause rather than the canned variety, but not until they'd ironed out creepy kinks like this.

Love Isn't Easy (But It Sure Is Hard Enough)

Benny Hill lives! For all the famed Abba "innocence", could it be that there's a smutty double entendre in there on a par with The Bellamy Brothers' highly witty "If I Said You Had A Beautiful Body, Would You Hold It Against Me?" Say it ain't so!

"Love Isn't Easy" is a straightforward enough slice of wannabe country-rock until crashing guitar chords and the girls' backing vocals swoop in on the line, "Now look at that guy." Which is where all Abba archaeologists get excitable. Because here, undeniably, is the first sighting of the seed that later grows into "Mamma Mia", or at least that savage hookline of "One more look"... Once again, *Ring Ring* is an album that isn't great in itself, but serves as a stepping-stone to eventual greatness.

This track in itself has a strong chorus, but sonically there's a discernible straining for effect which doesn't quite hack it. It's further proof that Benny and Bjorn didn't soar until the girls came on board. Lyrically, there are more ropey moments: a couple feud, the male bemoans how many presents he's bought the woman, and she replies: "Now listen to that/ Just look at that cat/ You'd think he was an angel, but he's talking through his hat." Did we say ropey? What we actually meant was genius, obviously.

Me and Bobby and Bobby's Brother

Hmm. After the last few, you could begin to wonder if the young Abba were ever clumsy with song titles…

Frida's solo spot, this one, and the already-experienced chanteuse gives it such commitment that she almost convinces you there are layers of depth and meaning to the song. One of the few lyrics solely penned by Benny (it wasn't long before he happily relinquished the wordsmith stuff to Bjorn), this nostalgic flashback finds Frida pining for childhood days, where she and Bobby and his bro played gaily together. There were of course fights and rows now and again, but mostly these idealised kids had a blast. The sun shone, the apple tree grew. How Frida wishes she could go back to that time. It doesn't appear to bother her that "They would take me out for football games and such/ They liked to play and I guess I didn't like it very much/ But anyway, I was happy and proud to be with the boys, being a little girl…"

"THERE WERE OF COURSE FIGHTS AND ROWS NOW AND AGAIN, BUT MOSTLY THESE IDEALISED KIDS HAD A BLAST."

Would it be too pompous to once again point out the recurring reasoning on this album that to be a girl, as opposed to a boy, is bad and feeble? Is somehow lesser, and small? Is that just a sign of those times? Or a Swedish thing? Are we reading too much into some harmless throwaway pop lyrics? And anyway, shouldn't we be saving this rant for the crowning glory of "I Am Just A Girl"?

He Is Your Brother

With obvious similarities thematically to "People Need Love", not to mention The Hollies' Neil Diamond-penned hit "He Ain't Heavy, He's My Brother", this is another case of a lacklustre rhythm track exposing the boys' slim vocals. The whole track sounds like it was recorded in, and by, a cement mixer, and the lumpen rhythm is something you never hear much outside Dennis Waterman and Chas'n'Dave singles, or cheap Ealing comedies where people's clothes fall off in a hilarious manner. Funky and sexy it isn't. It's very, very white. It oompahs, then oompahs again, and suggests we all stop fighting and feed the poor hungry beggars in the street.

Yet "He Is Your Brother", for all its schmaltz, does have some redeeming qualities. The opening piano lick is a little "Dancing Queen", and the boy/girl call and response technique deployed for the phrase "on the road" is a spiritual forerunner of that used later in arguably the most crucial song of their entire career, "S.O.S.", which brought them back to the big time after a post-"Waterloo" lull. But we're jumping ahead of ourselves…

And if the song as a whole reeks of Sandie Shaw

and Lulu singing "Puppet On A String" and "Boom Bang-A-Bang" at the same time, there's an extraordinary high-pitched yell of "Brother!!!" on the fade-out which is spookily out of context, fascinating, and kind of sci-fi. Weird.

She's My Kind Of Girl

A slightly more meaty male vocal this time, with shades of various Sixties hits in the melody: perhaps Bjorn and Benny had been spinning something by The Move, Love Affair, Gary Puckett and The Union Gap or Simon Dupree and The Big Sound? They don't attain that level of "epic", but it's an honest enough stab at it, and the production is smart.

> "PRIVATELY, ABBA WEREN'T TOO THRILLED BY THE SONG. TO BJORN AND BENNY IT REPRESENTED A BEST-FORGOTTEN PHASE IN THEIR CAREER."

This song, as we've discussed, already had something of a history, playing its part in the coming together of Abba. On the original Swedish release of the album, it was left off, in favour of fitting in both versions of the title track, but it made it off the subs' bench for the release internationally. How could the Brits, for example, not succumb to the charms of a song initially composed for *The Seduction Of Inga* (director: Joseph W. Sarno)? Its melancholy tune had already, as we've said, wooed the Japanese as a flukey number one hit for "Bjorn and Benny". (In fact it was to remain their biggest hit in that territory for years to come…)

Privately, Abba weren't too thrilled by the song. To Bjorn and Benny it represented a best-forgotten phase in their career. They'd felt "reduced" to it when the hits weren't flowing. They'd fretted that they were gradually becoming "former" pop stars. Up-and-coming stars Agnetha and Frida weren't keen on it either, especially as Agnetha knew Bjorn had been offered – and considered – an acting part in the movie, which wasn't an area she wanted her new husband to explore. Contrary to mythology, not every Swedish person wakes up and decides to make a blue movie every day…

I Am Just a Girl

Just a girl? Is that all? "Inferior" like, say, 51% of the world's population? Suspect ideology aside (we were kidding about the rant), "I Am Just A Girl" is a hummable tune, originally written for a movie and sung by a Swedish (male) actor. The same backing track from his session, that Bjorn and Benny had produced, was even re-used. In Japan,

fella smiles and whispers and looks her way. The shrinking violet, wallflower theme is a little patronising towards all single women, nevertheless. Or could the self-deprecation and self-pity of the narrator be the forerunner of the opening lines of "Thank You For The Music"? In which case, everything's forgiven!

Rock'n'Roll Band

Which rocks with all the blood'n'thunder authenticity of Timmy Mallett hosting *Songs Of Praise*. Rock'n'roll doesn't get much more wimpy than this. It wants to bang its head, but doesn't want to get a nasty graze. It is less ballsy – even – than Elton John's "Saturday Night's Alright For Fighting" or The Moody Blues' "I'm Just A Singer In A Rock'n'Roll Band". No, it was to be some time before Abba kicked like the wanton phallic hellbeasts we find on "Does Your Mother Know?"…

it was preferred by the record company as a single to "Ring, Ring", and scraped the top twenty there.

If it reminds you of something, that'll be Manhattan Transfer's chart-topping lounge ballad "Chanson D'Amour", a U.K. number one for three weeks in 1977. (Knocked off the top, incidentally, by "Knowing Me Knowing You".)

And although she's just a girl – "one among the others, nothing much to say, plain and simple" – this "Miss Nobody" decides life begins when her

Still, they practise their guitar chugging here, do that pre-chorus extra-loud chug which was to serve them in good stead later, and would sound like they were having fun if the boys' singing wasn't so weedy. The cut had been a Japanese b-side (to

"Love Has Its Ways") prior to this incarnation – it was re-jigged to fill up the album. Bjorn and Benny's lack of presence again highlights what a difference Agnetha and Frida were about to make to their sound. Time and again, this album shows that Abba may have ideas, talent, versatility and energy, but Bjorn and Benny didn't yet know how best to channel it. Michael Tretow was working wonders at the mixing desk, but he features on some tracks and not on others. Once the band members' gifts were harnessed, and the females gave them a whole new set of options, they'd be a force to be reckoned with, with the tireless Tretow coming into his own.

"Rock'N'Roll Band" urges us to "dance to the rock'n'roll band" (at least it doesn't claim that they *are* one), and not to "hide behind the flowers". What kind of rip-roaring, no-holds-barred "rock" event do you find flowers at? Grandma's party?

> "THIS ALBUM SHOWS THAT ABBA MAY HAVE IDEAS, TALENT, VERSATILITY AND ENERGY, BUT BJORN AND BENNY DIDN'T YET KNOW HOW BEST TO CHANNEL IT."

BONUS TRACKS on 2001 reissue:

Merry-Go-Round

The "Oriental" motif of this oh-gosh-I'm-so-lonely ditty shows how important the Japanese market was to the boys during this period, but it flopped there despite the Japanese record company's enthusiasm. The lame duck chorus tells you why. It made the b-side of "People Need Love" in Sweden.

Santa Rosa

The b-side to "He Is Your Brother" in Sweden, this began life as "Grandpa's Banjo" – yes, it really did – but thankfully Bjorn and Benny saw fit to change the lyrics. They tried to push it in Japan, no-one liked it, and even its writers later conceded that they didn't think much of it. Funny, really, as it's a pleasant, Byrds-lite number, reminiscent of Christie's hit "Yellow River" and featuring a catchy "ba ba ba" refrain not a million miles from The Kinks' "David Watts". It would have been boosted greatly by the girls' participation. The brief guitar-picking intro suggests somebody involved had heard George Harrison's "Here Comes The Sun"...

Ring, Ring
(Swedish Version)

Which sounds just as much fun in Swedish, and, unless you're Swedish, you can make up your own words when you sing along. Neil Sedaka's accountant presumably prefers the English version.

WATERLOO 1974

WATERLOO

SITTING IN THE PALMTREE

KING KONG SONG

HASTA MANANA

MY MAMA SAID

DANCE (WHILE THE MUSIC STILL GOES ON)

HONEY, HONEY

WATCH OUT

WHAT ABOUT LIVINGSTONE

GONNA SING YOU MY LOVE SONG

SUZY-HANG-AROUND

Bonus tracks on 2001 reissue:

RING, RING (US REMIX)

WATERLOO (SWEDISH)

HONEY HONEY (SWEDISH)

Recorded, September 1973 - February 1974, at Metronome, Stockholm.

Produced by Benny Andersson and Bjorn Ulvaeus. Engineered by Michael B. Tretow.

Musicians: Bjorn Ulvaeus (acoustic guitar), Benny Andersson (piano, moog, mellotron), Janne Schaffer (guitars), Rutger Gunnarsson (bass), Ola Brunkert (drums), Per Sahlberg (bass on "Dance"), Christer Eklund (tenor sax on "Waterloo"), Malandro Gassama (congas on "Sitting In The Palmtree"), Sven-Olof Walldoff (string arrangement on "Honey Honey").

Vocals by Abba.

W*ATERLOO* WAS THE FIRST ALBUM BY ABBA, AS OPPOSED TO THE FIRST ALBUM BY BJORN, BENNY, AGNETHA AND ANNI-FRID. THAT LENGTHY LIST OF FIRST NAMES WAS GETTING TO BE A MOUTHFUL EVEN FOR SWEDISH RADIO JOCKS, AND WASN'T EXACTLY CRYING OUT TO CATCH ON IN THE US OR UK. IT'D JUST BEEN HANDY, SHORT-TERM, TO TAG THE GIRLS' NAMES ONTO THE ALREADY "ESTABLISHED" DUO OF BLOKES.

Manager Stig now realised something more zestful was required. Fiddling around with the gang's initials one day, he settled on Abba. The group hesitated: Abba was also the name of a well-known Swedish canned fish company. It could be the equivalent of a British band naming themselves, say, Bird's Eye, or

HP. You can be *too* post-modern...The fish company gave their okay to the notion, though, and the band decided it was at least a better, more commercial-sounding moniker than Abraham, Martin, John, Peter, Paul, Mary, Old Uncle Tom Cobbley and all...

Erring on the side of caution, they labelled the subsequent *Waterloo* album and single as by Abba (Bjorn, Benny, Agnetha & Frida)...

Like *Ring, Ring, Waterloo* was precipitated by Sweden's national obsession with the Eurovision Song Contest. The previous year's humiliation hadn't put the group off – in fact, they were keener than ever and determined to prove a point. And they were encouraged by the jury this time round being made up of members of the public rather than music biz "experts", and knew that the only way around the disdain that Americans and British generally showed to Swedish pop was through the mass exposure of Eurovision. If they wanted to cross over, they *needed* Eurovision "glory".

At the time, the group were only playing live shows at weekends, because of Agnetha's maternal commitments, so Bjorn and Benny had plenty of time to write. Or they *would* have had, were it not for their day jobs helping Stig run the Polar organisation. Their hearts set on getting second time lucky and penning a Eurovision winner, the two men took off to their summer houses in Viggso, an island in the

Stockholm archipelago, where they'd begun to hide out for uninterrupted, distraction-free, song-writing sessions. And a loosening-up drink or two.

Let's not forget, Bjorn and Benny still harboured an image of themselves as "rock'n'rollers" – it took years for them to accept that they were perceived as cuddly bland uncle figures the world over, and had best get used to it if they wanted the cheques to keep rolling in.

Another oft-perpetuated rumour had Agnetha and Frida, if not at each others' throats, at least just tolerating each other for the sake of band morale and their marriages. Unlike their men, they weren't natural, instinctive friends or colleagues. Agnetha was a flirtatious onstage presence and sex symbol; Frida was an old school, more "formal" vocalist. Agnetha was riddled with insecurities, only too ready to sacrifice her personal ambitions to go along with Bjorn's vision, and later developed a full-blown Greta Garbo complex. Years on, she even had a serious relationship with a stalker of hers, which ended in a court case.

Frida was mature beyond her years, earnest and professional. She knew what she wanted, whereas Agnetha wasn't sure. Frida's relationship with Benny was at this time stable; Agnetha's with Bjorn was already volatile if passionate. The four had blazing rows and belly laughs, yet soon twigged that the popular image of four wholesome happy shiny touchy-feely Swedes was a big portion of their mega-meal ticket…

For now, however, the eyes of the four were on the big prizes. Bjorn and Benny focussed on conjuring up that song that would render global resistance futile. They'd happily jam for hours, just trading licks on guitar and piano, tossing around ideas, rejecting some, nurturing others. They (and close ally engineer Michael Tretow) were still heavily influenced by Phil Spector's Sixties work, and by West Coast US soft rock. The British glam rock sound was seeping into their consciousness, too.

> "BJORN AND BENNY STILL HARBOURED AN IMAGE OF THEMSELVES AS 'ROCK'N'ROLLERS' - IT TOOK YEARS FOR THEM TO ACCEPT THAT THEY WERE PERCEIVED AS CUDDLY BLAND UNCLE FIGURES THE WORLD OVER"

One of their efforts, deemed sparky and catchy, was committed to cassette, with humming in place of words, and forwarded to guru Stig, who'd enjoyed a tidy sideline for over a decade as one of the country's most productive lyricists. See what you can come up with for this, they suggested.

Stig at first played around with the phrase "honey pie", but nothing gelled. He wanted something that'd make sense the world over, nothing too esoteric or tough to translate. The goal was perfect pop, after all, not Pulitzer-winning literature. Flicking through a book of famous quotations he was captivated by the idea of Napoleon Bonaparte, and the diminutive dictator's ultimate defeat in 1815 at the hands of the British and Germans. This historic battle occurred in a Belgian town. The town was called Waterloo.

While this may disappoint those of you who thought the song was about a railway station just south of central London, it worked for everyone else. Stig's interest in history meant that for his budding protégés Abba the rest, too, was history… The girl in the song surrenders to her suitor, and at the same time the world surrendered to a euphoric, ecstatic pop song.

"Hasta Manana" gave it a run for its money, but at the eleventh hour the team decided on "Waterloo", wanting to submit a less obvious entry to the national Eurovision panel – who, they hoped, were tiring of the traditional melodramatic ballad format by now. It featured the two girls' vocals combined as opposed to Agnetha solo, and Stig promised the band they could "slit his throat" if it was the wrong call. Maybe "Ring, Ring" hadn't been a total failure. Maybe it'd battered at the doors, and those doors were now ready to open.

It was, indeed, Sesame time! In February 1974 Abba won the Swedish heats by a mile. "The voice of the people", declared the newspapers. "At last – the best song wins", they hollered. And, "This time

the right song won!" The public knew a top tune when they heard one. Abba, the accompanying album in the bag and set for a March release, started trying on their glitziest glad rags, preparing to take Eurovision 1974 to be held in Brighton, England, by storm. Finally facing their very own Waterloo, they were about to win a crucial battle.

Waterloo

My, my. Abba's first British chart-topper (they went on to have no less than nine), the unforgettable "Waterloo" was, therefore, Bjorn and Benny's second stab at writing a Eurovision Song Contest winner. If Napoleon Bonaparte hasn't featured before or since in many classic pop songs, the British and international record-buying publics followed his example and capitulated, or "did surrender", to its rollicking hooklines. It was to be the last time anyone needed to explain exactly who Abba were. Our fate was to be with them.

As the band were recording the Waterloo album, during late 1973 to early '74, it soon became clear that this was a stand-out number. For a short while the broody ballad sung by Agnetha, "Hasta Manana", had been some band members' favourite for the Eurovision slot, but "Waterloo" won the day. The fact that it pushed both Agnetha and Frida to the fore better served the group's efforts to establish their image as a glammy yet wholesome foursome. The eyes of the world would be watching Eurovision: Abba, no mugs, wanted to sell themselves as much as any single song. They may be singing, "I feel like I win when I lose", but after years of hard work in the industry, their hearts

were set on those glittering prizes.

On April 6, 1974, Abba stormed the Eurovision stage in cosmopolitan Brighton, a riot of colour, tinsel and innocent yet sexy energy. "Waterloo" was the first ever Swedish winner, and arguably the most memorable moment in Eurovision's entire history (though Lulu, Johnny Logan, Bucks Fizz and Dana – and for that matter, Dana International – might, in all subjectivity, beg to differ). It locked Abba into the minds of viewers: in terms of their costumes, presentation and pizzazz they had to be larger than life from this point onwards. Their knack for pure pop, however, meant they were rarely to lapse into pretension or bombast.

Soon the song had hit number one in Britain, Ireland, West Germany, Belgium and Norway, gone top five in countless other countries, and reached number six in America. In the UK it shot to number one for two weeks (displacing Terry Jacks' "Seasons In The Sun" and in turn being displaced by The Rubettes' "Sugar Baby Love"). It was the sixteenth biggest-selling single of the year (other big singles acts of '74 included Mud ("Tiger Feet" was the end-of-year champ), Paper Lace, George McCrae, Alvin Stardust and David Essex. And, er, The Wombles. Of Wimbledon Common were they.)

Contrary to popular rose-tinted memory, Abba didn't capitalise immediately. In fact they had eighteen nervous months of rocky commercial uncertainty (and relative flops such as "Honey Honey", "So Long", and "I Do I Do I Do I Do I Do") before "S.O.S." and "Mamma Mia" propelled them back to the top of the pop pile in '75.

Yet on that fateful April day in 1974, all Abba were concerned about was whether Brighton was ready to rock…

The odds on their winning had recently dropped from 6/1 favourites to 20/1 outsiders, and one English newspaper had captioned their photograph "no-hopers". "Waterloo" was being played on the radio a lot though, at least as much as the British entry, Olivia Newton-John singing "Long Live Love".

After attending music biz parties in London, Abba arrived in Brighton on Tuesday 2 April to find they were staying at the Grand Hotel's "Napoleon" suite. An omen, surely, or perhaps another cunning Stig manoeuvre? They checked out the Dome Theatre, where the contest was to take place.

In rehearsals, they realised their pre-recorded backing track, over which they were to sing live on the Saturday, was much too quiet. The British technicians refused to turn it up until Stig had an embarrassing, but highly effective, hissy fit.

Friday night, and Abba toasted Agnetha's 24th birthday with champagne. It had been a stressful week of interviews, photo shoots and rehearsals, but they were relatively confident. Stig regularly gave them morale-boosting lectures. Bjorn and Frida went for a quiet meal, Bjorn and Agnetha for a leisurely stroll around Brighton.

Saturday, and the incomparable Katie Boyle is presenting the show. Sweden's representatives are eighth to perform. Five hundred million people are watching on television. Abba, practically showbiz veterans despite their youth, shake off any nerves and give it their all. Their tight pants, platform boots, jewels and stars and glitter are a refreshing, exuberant, cack-handed take on the glam rock images currently prevalent in British pop circles…

"THE JUDGING BEGINS, AND ABBA ARE IMMEDIATELY GIVEN MAXIMUM POINTS BY FINLAND. ENGLAND GIVES THEM NONE…"

" ...BUT AS THE VOTING CLIMAXES, FIVE POINTS FROM THE SWISS MEANS ABBA CAN'T LOSE. "

The judging begins, and Abba are immediately given maximum points by Finland. England gives them none. But as the voting climaxes, five points from the Swiss means Abba can't lose. Italy's Gigliola Cinquetti's "Si" is second, Holland's Mouth & MacNeal, with "I See A Star", (later a minor British hit) come third. It's a piquant result, as the night before a drunken Mouth had taunted the Swedes with inebriated boasts about his imminent victory. Bjorn, Benny, Agnetha and Frida hug and jump for joy. When the prize is handed to the song's writers, Stig is onstage for some time, not shy in making speeches, before Bjorn and Benny can convince the over-zealous bouncers that they're legit and are permitted to join him. Abba trot through the winning song one more time, to scenes of euphoria. There's a sense that this marks a new era in Eurovision, that this surge of vibrant pop marks the death knell of the sentimental ballad. (Of course it doesn't. At least, not for long.)

Among the stream of innocuous, happy inter-

view questions, one journalist asks: "Do you realise that forty thousand men died in the Battle of Waterloo?" "Why do you have to politicise every-thing?" snaps a bemused Stig. Abba are prevailed upon to party till 6a.m. They awake next morning to a deluge of congratulations, offers and requests, and the realisation that they've arrived on the global scene and things will never be the same again. The next day, they drive to London for more promo, including a memorable first *Top Of The Pops* appearance and a photo call at a London railway station. See if you can guess which one, readers.

The photogenic qualities of Agnetha in particular do not go unnoticed. The Swedish ambassador gets in on the act: "This is my proudest day in England. You're all fine ambassadors." By Wednesday 10th, after so many interviews, Agnetha's developed a throat problem, but the team fulfills TV engagements in Holland and Germany before taking a well-earned Easter break in Viggso. They see their kids, take a deep breath, and, now that it's guaranteed, wonder what inter-national fame is going to mean to them.

A hit album, just for starters. Much better produced than *Ring Ring*, the *Waterloo* album is an odd mix of lush pop and quirky comedy songs. It sounds as if Abba are still learning their strengths and weaknesses, but learning fast. They're learning that the girls' vocals are essential, that they can come up with a glam rock flourish or two, that they're capable of doing intriguing, rather than stereotypical, things with big epic love songs, and that they still have hidden reserves to tap into. They're still a long way from peaking, but the extremes of both sangfroid and silliness here show that they're not afraid to extend their reach.

Sitting In The Palmtree

If "Waterloo" itself is two minutes and forty six seconds of irresistible pop, with its method of accentuating chord changes with piano notes a device they'd tap into forevermore, its perfection isn't realised on every album track. Not yet. "Waterloo" boasts an addictive guitar chug, lovely sax (influenced perhaps by Roy Wood's Wizzard), handclaps that match the stomping (lack of) subtlety of The Sweet or Mud (or any Mike Chapman/ Nicky Chinn production), and sky-high backing vocals. Years later, its blend of sounds was to influence everyone from Madonna ("Holiday") to Elvis Costello ("Oliver's Army").

"Sitting In The Palmtree", however, is a dodgy cod-reggae number, and something of a disaster. It highlights how Abba were trying everything at this stage and maybe how lucky they were to hit on "Waterloo". They were versatile, yes, but they weren't yet enlightened as to their best route. After success, the public kind of showed them the way to go.

> "THEY WERE VERSATILE, YES, BUT THEY WEREN'T YET ENLIGHTENED AS TO THEIR BEST ROUTE. AFTER SUCCESS, THE PUBLIC KIND OF SHOWED THEM THE WAY TO GO."

It's hard to imagine a more disappointing second track. Anyone purchasing the *Waterloo* album on the back of the breakthrough hit – i.e. everyone who bought it – must have been perplexed. If this was the second track, they'd have thought, no wonder the Swedes struggled to find a follow-up hit. (Ironic, of course, given our perception now of

Abba as machine-like hit-purveyors). With congas, featherweight "dub" rhythms and an embarrassing attempt to emulate the sound made when coconuts are clip-clopped together, "Palmtree" is reggae like S Club 7 are heavy metal. The male vocal is excruciatingly bloodless (and oh-so-white), and the groove paper-thin. Only the entrance of the girls for a sonorous middle eight gives it a lift, but it soon reverts to its – for want of a better word – "feel". Reggae, unsurprisingly, was never to be Abba's forte – not in this or any other year. Not on this or any other planet.

And those words! What were thinking? Evidently having enjoyed a half of lager too many, our narrator fancies himself sat up a tree "among his coconuts". "People laugh and point their fingers, like I was a monkey at the zoo." Suspect? Stoned? Or just plain silly?

One of the last songs recorded for the album, and *not* one of the all-time Abba greats.

King Kong Song

It get sillier... oh dear. What an extraordinarily unflattering running order this album revels in, with all of (well, most of) its turkeys placed proudly up at the top table. At best, "King Kong Song" is a hummable Beach Boys pastiche. At worst, it's the product of a completely and utterly burned-out lyricist, bereft of inspiration and desperately noting down what he's just been watching on the telly. It begins: "Well I was looking at a movie on the TV last night/Then I had a very funny notion, yeah/ I really had to write a song about it/ And then I'm gonna sing it with my rock'n'roll band..."

Not content with this confession, it adds: "And I bet the people gonna like it, yeah!"

How much are you willing to wager, then?

The song goes on to name-check King Kong lots of times, for no special reason. It reckons it's "kinda funky", and urges: "Let your arms hang down and waddle all around/Like a dreadful mighty killer, a big black wild gorilla..."

Hmmm... when did workaholics Bjorn and Benny find the time to watch so much telly, anyway? If it was addling their brains, at least it wasn't hindering their musical gifts so badly. "King Kong Song", despite the lyrics from hell, isn't such a bad "rock'n'roll" number, if you're generous with your definitions of "rock'n'roll". Let's face it, Abba were *never* Led Zeppelin, but this has a great, crunchy guitar intro. Again, that career-defining device of emphasising chord changes on Benny's piano is employed. And again the boys' vocals are vapid. A "pap ooh mow mow"-style backing refrain pushes things along.

> "*KING KONG* SONG, DESPITE THE LYRICS FROM HELL, ISN'T SUCH A BAD 'ROCK'N'ROLL' NUMBER."

When the girls take over for the second verse, it's blatantly clear how much matters improve. By now it must have been obvious to everyone in the world apart from Bjorn and Benny and Stig that Abba sounded better with the girls more involved. They refresh parts of Abba songs that Bjorn and Benny can't reach. Though the track still resolutely refuses to get off the runway, there are even some screams – ooh, look, a gorilla! – towards the end.

It's conceivable that Abba had heard one or two of Manchester band 10CC's more "wacky" moments (and misunderstood their intellectual intent) here, and the riff echoes those Chinnichap combos (Sweet, Mud, Suzi Quatro, etc) again – it's a very of-its-time, hot-pants-and-platform-boots riff. Nevertheless, game though it is, "King Kong Song" remains more Fay Wray (make that Fey Wray) than Link Wray.

You'd have thought they were a bunch of zany, clueless Scandinavian one-hit wonders, not the group who were to become the decade's most viable pop force…

Hasta Mañana

A touch of class, at last. Reeling as we are from all the preceding wackiness, "Hasta Manana" – so nearly the Eurovision entry, and then how differently would things have turned out? – comes as a relief. It's a big floaty ballad, sung by Agnetha. The horses' hooves rhythm again betrays the boys' Hootenanny/Hep Stars roots; it was only once they'd shaken those off that Abba became truly Abba, the well-oiled, cosmopolitan hit machine.

Stig had fallen in love with a random Spanish phrase while on holiday, hearing it everywhere, and the working title of "Who's Gonna Love You?" was binned. (Coincidentally, American duo Sparks used it around the same time in the track, "Hasta Mañana, Monsieur"). The chorus is very Eurovision, with just a hint of the Everly Brothers' classic "Walk Right Back" sneaking in there. The section where Agnetha breaks off to speak the lyrics – "where is the dream we were dreaming?" – is meant to be touching, and is.

Polar discovery Lena Andersson had a Swedish number one with it in 1975. Two and a half decades later, sexed-up Euro-disco outfit Army Of Lovers covered the song. "Hasta Mañana"'s main claim to fame, however, will always involve "what if?" If Abba had gone with it instead of "Waterloo" in April '74, would pop history, in that parallel dimension, have been very different? Or massively different? Would we have even heard of Abba?

"THE CHORUS IS VERY EUROVISION, WITH JUST A HINT OF THE EVERLY BROTHERS' CLASSIC *WALK RIGHT BACK* SNEAKING IN THERE."

My Mama Said

One of the album's best and most durable tracks, "My Mama Said" finds Abba honing a fuller, richer sound. They set out to be funky, sexy, almost jazzy, and – incredibly – are. The guitar licks are slick and tasteful and the clipped grooving over the fade is almost in the league of the masters of that genre, Nile Rodgers and Bernard Edwards' Chic. The bassline ripples, everything about it is – dare we say it – cool.

Production as fine as this shines a light on the way forward for Abba. Their future sheen and their superb way of painting with gloss is all previewed here. They're not tinny any more. The girls sound like sex sliding about on more sex, and it's the first Abba album track that makes you wish it went on longer – and it could have done, with grace and impunity.

> "PRODUCTION AS FINE AS THIS SHINES A LIGHT ON THE WAY FORWARD FOR ABBA."

Lyrically, it's another of those glance-back-at-the-traumas-of-adolescence stories Bjorn and Benny seemed to enjoy writing. The female narrator's mum won't let her slip out to meet her boyfriend, telling her to stay in and make her bed, because "Pa and me, we give you room and bread". Our heroine just wants to go out and "live her life". What teenager doesn't? Arguably, her mum is a bit over-dramatic when she sighs, "I suppose you'd rather see me dead". A corking track. A revelation.

Dance (While the Music Still Goes On)

The influence of Phil Spector on Bjorn, Benny and Michael Tretow has never been made more explicit than on this lovely, elevating track, which emphatically places a grin in your heart. Once again, it's a shame the boys don't just leave the vocals to Frida, but the production makes this swing, with panache. And it's not just a wall-of-sound rip-off: there's a uniquely Abba-esque quality to those piano and guitar fills. Like all the best chord sequences, this one feels inevitable…

The echo-ey drumbeat, laced with cowbells and chimes, immediately brings to mind The Ronettes, The Crystals, classic pop nuggets like "Be My Baby" and The Beach Boys' "Don't Worry Baby". There's something festive about the track, or maybe it's just that that Spector sparkle brings to mind all his Christmas greats, like "Frosty The Snowman". Frida and Agnetha can carry off the Ronnie Spector high notes too, even if the boys patently cannot.

It's lyrically another tale of love facing extinction – "our love was a snowbird, it's flying away" – and has a genuine emotional verve. Polar-signed duo Svenne & Lotta, produced by Bjorn and Benny, released their version as an Australian single.

And if throughout their career Abba were often

Honey Honey

It seemed this song was destined to be a hit... as long as you weren't Abba. Footnotes-to-pop-history Sweet Dreams, an English duo, took it into the UK top ten in August 1974. Yet when Abba released it as a single Stateside, as a follow-up to "Waterloo", it stalled at number 27. A respectable placing, but hardly world domination: hopes had been high. And the UK follow-up "Ring, Ring" – refurbished one more time – didn't help matters, peaking outside the top thirty, its chances adversely affected by a technicians' strike just when they were booked to plug it on *Top Of The Pops*.

"Honey, Honey" made the top five in Spain, Germany and Switzerland, but didn't prove to be the earth-mover Abba wanted. Yet pop doesn't get much more delightfully direct and catchy. It may be inane, but it's also insanely memorable once that nursery-rhyme melody sinks its claws into you. And it's one of the few times that Agnetha and Frida allow themselves to be overtly, rather than implicitly, sexy. The saucy, sub-*Carry On* lyrics aren't exactly erotic, but what the Swedes do with them is. "How you thrill me... now I know what they mean, you're a love machine" is one thing; "Honey, to say the least, you're a doggone beast" is quite another. There are even some spells of subliminal heavy breathing as our cheerleader recites these come-ons to her man. Of course, the fun and frolics drop like a stone when the boys butt in for the middle eight – it rather kills the otherwise willing suspension of disbelief. But it picks up again, with Spector-style "Ba ba ba"s and repetitions, and hints of Mac And Katie Kissoon's hits such as "Sugar Candy Kisses". Sweet.

to be pilloried by po-faced rock critics, for being overly "commercial", this song (and indeed, this album) drew a heap of healthy praise from no less credible a source than *Rolling Stone* magazine. Their reviewer Ken Barnes wrote: "(The band's) emergence is one of the most cheering musical events in recent months... With their concise, upbeat pop creations, Abba is much closer to the essential spirit of rock'n'roll than any number of hotshot guitarists or devotional ensembles handing down cosmo-dynamic enlightenment to the huddled masses". Whew!

Watch Out

Woah! Abba get down'n'dirty and *rock*! Or seem to think they do...

Quite the most startling, eyebrow-raising track on the album (arguably on *any* Abba album), "Watch Out" is the chaps' sadly blatant stab at displaying how hard they are. Black Sabbath, Led Zeppelin, Hawkwind? Bjorn and Benny have 'for breakfast... in their dreams!

The fuzzy guitar riff is a shot at heavy metal, and Bjorn's record collection at the time must have featured an album or two by Jimi Hendrix, Eric Clapton or Jeff Beck. And by Abba standards, it's very grungey and grubby. You just have to love it. Curb that smirk.

With Bjorn and Benny working out a few long-haired frustrations, it's Abba as the "rock'n'roll band" their lyrics keep bizarrely purporting them to be. Foxy bassline, beefy drums – the other musicians obviously kept their mouths shut, winked at each other, and had a damn good time. It makes you want to jump up and down, pour lighter fluid on your head and annoy the neighbours at maximum volume.

And that explosion at the end! A rip-off of UK glitter-kids The Sweet and their fantastic 1973 hit "Hellraiser", surely? Overall, in truth, "Watch Out" more closely resembles one of The Sweet's more dodgy, self-penned b-sides. But let's not knock what is a real Abba rarity. Here, and debatably here alone, Abba actually kick serious ass. Okay, maybe not serious ass, but ass of a sort, certainly. "I'm gonna tame you, wild thing." Yeeeeahh!! 'Scuse me while I go and bite the head off a goat, or something.

What About Livingstone

And just as the raw power is surging through our Satan-worshipping veins, *this* happens. Abba go all sweet and fluffy and coy again, with this slab of plinky-plonk prissiness which has the saving grace of at least being 100% barking mad. An odd, saccharin-sweet number, its lyrical concept tells of a man who, on hearing people diss the brave men we call astronauts, launches into a heartfelt homage to all the great explorers and pioneers of history – e.g. Professor Livingstone. Sadly the idea isn't matched by a sound that could in any way be described as exploratory or pioneering. Agnetha and Frida try a few more Ronettes tropes, but their hearts aren't in it.

"What About Livingstone" makes you think it was written on the way to the newsagent to buy a paper. "Went to buy me a paper at the local news-stand..." Ah, hang on, it *was*.

And who laughs at astronauts anyway? Swedes are *weird*.

Gonna Sing You My Love Song

Abba return to some grown-up dignity here, with the chanteuses singing (their love song) serenely, and everyone piling in for the big chorus. The backing, though, is restrained and cleverly structured, and carries a strong song along nicely. Bjorn and Benny are beginning to learn that what you leave out is as important as what you put in. The musicians are developing an understanding, a rapport, even if Frida lapses into her cruise ship entertainer mode at times. There's a warm guitar coda, and the glimpses of grandeur would make for a suitable album finale for any sensible, one-dimensional band. But this is Abba we're talking about, and so…

Suzy-Hang-Around

Like the previous album's "Me And Bobby And Bobby's Brother", this rare example of Benny writing the lyrics and singing solo is a nostalgic reminiscence, Suzy being a young girl who wasn't allowed to play with the older boys, when "she was nine and I was ten". Having banished poor Suzy from the playground, the story then leaves her hanging for all eternity, Benny failing to provide any kind of resolution or ending to the fable. We want closure!

And was he familiar with Glen Campbell's "Where's The Playground, Susie?" by any remote chance? Eventually, Benny was to concede that he was a much slower – and less able – lyricist than Bjorn, and leave his colleague to it. It's clear throughout this album that lyrics were at this point an afterthought, deemed almost a nuisance once you'd come up with a snappy title. Like, er, "What About Livingstone". As often as we tend to say "thank you for the music" with reference to Abba, we should be mightily grateful the godawful lyrics improved as they went on…

The guitars here, however, are lovely. From the off, acoustics and electrics are merged West Coast-style, giving the song a light Byrds/Crosby Stills Nash & Young vibe, the kind of feel later

mastered by Tom Petty and The Heartbreakers. It's interesting to hear the Abba men showing off their versatility again – if thoroughly out of context with the rest of the *Waterloo* album. Needless to say, Benny's vocals (check out that pronunciation of "har-mow-nee-ee" – ouch) are those of a drunk playing the comb through crepe paper.

But then, what is "in context" for the *Waterloo* album? A deranged mishmash of glam rock, hard rock, soft ballads and schlock-schmaltz (oh, and cod reggae), it's a one-off. Abba are still finding their way, feeling out the route to pop perfection. Soon, it'll all hang together. They hadn't known, recording this odd opus, that it'd be selling on the back of that smash hit breakthrough single. They may have dreamed of it. Now they were major international stars. All they had to do, these geniuses of hit making, was to consolidate and capitalise, ensure they weren't one-hit wonders. If anyone could come up with an instant follow-up, it was Abba, right?

Well, for a while as it happens, wrong. The next chapter in their history was supposed to be glorious for Abba – what they'd worked towards for so long. But it was to prove, for a worrying eighteen-month period, frustrating. The next hit wasn't to come tomorrow, or the day after. It wasn't to come until September 1975.

BONUS TRACKS on 2001 reissue:

Ring, Ring (US Remix)
Waterloo (Swedish)
Honey Honey (Swedish)

ABBA 1975

Recorded August 1974 - March 1975
at Glen, Metrodome and Ljudkopia, Stockholm.

Produced by Bjorn Ulvaeus and Benny
Andersson. Engineered by Michael B. Tretow.

Musicians: Bjorn Ulvaeus (guitars);
Benny Andersson (piano, clavinet, synthesisers);
Janne Schaffer (guitar); Finn Sjoberg (guitar);
Lasse Wellander (guitar); Rutger Gunnarsson
(bass); Mike Watson (bass); Ola Brunkert (drums);
Roger Palm (drums); Bruno Glenmark (trumpet);
Ulf Andersson (tenor sax, alto sax);
Sven-Olof Walldoff (string arrangements);
Bjorn Json Lindh (horn and sax arrangements).

Vocals by Abba.

MAMMA MIA

HEY, HEY HELEN

TROPICAL LOVELAND

S.O.S.

MAN IN THE MIDDLE

BANG-A-BOOMERANG

I DO, I DO, I DO, I DO, I DO

ROCK ME

INTERMEZZO NO. 1

I'VE BEEN WAITING FOR YOU

SO LONG

Bonus tracks on 2001 reissue:

CRAZY WORLD

**MEDLEY: PICK A BALE OF COTTON/ON
TOP OF OLD SMOKEY/MIDNIGHT SPECIAL**

Abba, holidaying, were happy. "Waterloo" had reached number one in England, Ireland, Germany, France, Austria, Denmark, Holland, Switzerland, Luxembourg, Belgium, Norway, Finland, Australia, and of course Sweden. It even made number six in the United States. After all Abba's hard work, here were the rewards. Surely a stream of hits would follow as surely as night follows day. What could possibly go wrong now?

Well, first of all, they made the classic and time-honoured mistake of upsetting the loyal followers of their formative years the minute they broke big. They outraged Sweden, which, when you think about it, takes some doing. Having agreed in January 1974 to take the traditional route of touring the country's "folk parks" through July, they cried off the commitment, claiming they now – as international hit-makers – had to reorganise their schedule. Media, business types and fans all howled with disgust. One folk park director captured the national mood when he declared that, "Abba's decision is terribly immoral. They have won an important international music competition with the Swedish people's support. Now they abandon their home audience completely to concentrate on the foreign market." Another roared, "This is the ugliest betrayal I've experienced in my many years in the business. I have engaged the

greatest stars in the entire world and now I am ridiculed by a group of Swedish amateurs, who I'm sure will be forgotten within the year."

Abba made some diplomatic redress by including dates across Sweden as part of their international tour, and of course the "betrayed" were soon onside again, talking up their own part in the Abba success story. (The following year the band insisted on atoning with several folk park gigs, despite the ever-ambitious Stig Anderson's protests.) Yet if Abba thought international hits were going to fall immediately into their hands on the back of "Waterloo", they were seriously wrong: they were to be frustrated in their increased ambitions for some time, particularly regarding their fortunes in the "home of pop music", Great Britain.

The promotion schedules, after that brief vacation, were hectic. The next album had to be recorded between trips to numerous countries, not to mention a Frida solo album, an Agnetha solo album, and Bjorn and Benny's production duties for other Polar acts. As the *ABBA* album came together, the teaser singles didn't clean up as anticipated. "So Long" flopped in Britain, where they were branded Eurovision one-hit wonders, and "I Do, I Do, I Do, I Do, I Do" fared equally poorly, although in Australia it proved a complete phenomenon. From then on, "Abba-mania" was rife in the land down under, and "Mamma Mia" was number one for a mighty eleven weeks. (A year later, all the Australian record company had to do was flip this single over, call the notional b-side "Rock Me" the a-side, and have it make the top three all over again.)

To Abba, "S.O.S." was the third single from the album, but to the U.K. it was the first that mattered, and the one which clinched their status as stars. A collective "phew" emerged from Abba's mouths and psyches. "S.O.S.", helped by zealous *Top Of The Pops* performances and much radio play, climbed to number six in September. "Mamma Mia" followed in January, giving them another number one – and this time, there was no going back. Now they couldn't release a flop if they tried.

"*SO LONG* FLOPPED IN BRITAIN, WHERE THEY WERE BRANDED EUROVISION ONE-HIT WONDERS, AND *I DO, I DO, I DO, I DO, I DO* FARED EQUALLY POORLY, ALTHOUGH IN AUSTRALIA IT PROVED A COMPLETE PHENOMENON."

The album was the group's first real international smash, topping charts everywhere from Norway to

Zimbabwe. In the U.K. it peaked at just number thir-teen (their last non-chart-topper for eight years). It was a decidedly odd year for albums, though. British album chart toppers ranged from Led Zeppelin to Max Boyce, from Elton John to The Stylistics, from Rod Stewart to Status Quo to Queen. Queen's flamboyant Christmas number one "Bohemian Rhapsody" was, you may remember, not averse to using the phrase "mamma mia". Abba's song replaced it at the top in January '76. Once more with feeling: my, my.

Around this time, prior to and during the album's and singles' release, Abba made the important move of linking up with director Lasse Hallstrom. Film footage wasn't called "videos" then: relatively unsophisticated, whatever "promo clips" Hallstrom could conjure up were sent off to the faraway TV stations which even hard-travelling Abba couldn't reach as easily as they'd like. These wowed the Aussies. Hallstrom was beginning to make a name for himself as a director – later of course he was to helm Abba's own movie. Later still, he was to become one of the world's most successful film-makers, the eye behind *The Cider House Rules, Chocolat, The Shipping News*, and others.

At this stage, he was "merely" a pioneer in the medium of "the video", which was to radically rearrange the pop landscape. Younger generations won't be able to imagine hearing a new pop record without seeing the accompanying video. They perhaps won't be able to imagine imagining. Hallstrom's teaming with Abba was serendipitous in the extreme. They now well and truly had their teeth into that pop landscape themselves. Their own long-fostered imaginings were becoming reality, sprinkled with a healthy dose of fantasy.

Gone were the chunky-knit cardigans and prissy suits. Abba had taken a shine to glam, and glam had left its sheen on them. Abba onstage were now choreographed and eye-catching. Bjorn and Benny sported glittery trousers and leopard skin jackets with élan. Agnetha's cat suits had taken to redefining the word "skin-tight". Her bottom was provoking gallons of slavering, admiring male comment when Kylie was a mere infant. Even the supposedly earnest Frida was rarely sighted wearing anything more modest than an incendiary mini-skirt. Confidence and commercial success were now encouraging Abba to rock like they'd always wanted to. They dared to be devilish.

Mamma Mia

From the pinpoint marimba tick-tock to the sus-penseful piano-and-guitar intro and the surging rhythmic rushes of the chorus, "Mamma Mia" is a textbook pop classic, stylishly structured. Abba again utilise – and now hone – their device of emphasising motifs and hooks with precise musical swoops, and by the time we get to "Just one look!" we're unable to get off the rollercoaster, even if we wanted to. Catchy as can be, the song – like "Hasta Mañana" – uses a well-known Euro-phrase (familiar during this period, as discussed above, thanks to Queen's "Bohemian Rhapsody") as a spine on which to hang its exuberant flesh. The Spector influence is still there in this song of a lover's irresistibility, and the arrangement milks every opportunity to provide the rush the listener gets when everything storms back in after cutting out momentarily. And the fade-out, forcing our attention towards that strange yet hypnotic guitar line, is haunting indeed…

Lyrically, some feel this – along with "S.O.S." – marks the first indications of Bjorn's awareness of cracks opening up in his relationship with Agnetha. There's plenty of contrary evidence, though, which says the couple were still very much in happy loved-up-bunnies mode at this stage. After all, their careers were going rather well…

Abba's second U.K. number one (the first of three consecutive), and an absolute monster in Australia, "Mamma Mia" wasn't even considered as a single in Britain until the Australians picked up on it. It also topped the charts in Germany and Switzerland. Years later, of course, it was the title of Abba's spin-off stage musical.

> " ABBA'S SECOND U.K. NUMBER ONE (THE FIRST OF THREE CONSECUTIVE), AND AN ABSOLUTE MONSTER IN AUSTRALIA. "

Lasse Hallstrom was working on a very small budget with the visuals. He'd often shoot two songs in a day. He had cut his teeth experimenting on TV, and was used to making things interesting through skilful editing and making-do. His "Mamma Mia" film marked the first use of what became his Abba trademark extreme close-ups of one or two band members, often in profile. Lips and eyes predominated. Agnetha and Frida looked like surreal clockwork poppets, or perhaps that should be puppets. Hallstrom would shoot two singles or pairs, then allow the viewer to compare and contrast, sometimes hitting on an inexplicable simple emotional resonance. In Australia, his clips caused a landslide of affection for the Swedes. Repeat on-air viewings were demanded. Abba had lit a fire within what passed as the Aussie soul.

Hey, Hey Helen

The *ABBA* album, like its predecessor *Waterloo*, is both delightful and frustrating in the way it shows Abba still finding out what was so great about themselves. For every pop classic, there's a berserk bit of nonsense. For every finely crafted, lovingly arranged slice of perfection, there's a dopey attempt to emulate another genre. Bjorn and Benny seem to want to keep trying to prove how versatile they are, whereas in fact what the listener wants is for them to be – purely and simply and gloriously – Abba. So at this point they're still mimicking other contemporary bands, displaying their (in)ability to do reggae or rock, refusing to see how streamlined they could be, striding eagerly up some blind alleys. You can't knock them for energy or curiosity. (In America, the album was promoted as "progressive rock". Uh-huh.)

"Hey, Hey Helen" is glitter rock. Not glam rock, but glitter rock. Different thing. Bowie and Bolan and Roxy Music had brought glam rock strutting

onto our speakers and screens. In their wake came a host of imitators, bandwagon-jumpers who diluted the mystique but took some thundering pop singles into the national consciousness to make up for it; Slade, Gary Glitter, The Glitter Band, Barry Blue and countless others. Greatest of these were the bands backed by aforementioned songwriting-producing team Nicky Chinn and Mike Chapman (later Blondie's producer), who included The Sweet, Mud and Suzi Quatro. Their stars were just – just – beginning to wane by late '75, but Abba had taken their cheeky cheap thrills on board. Some of these bands' power-packing records – "Ballroom Blitz", "Hellraiser", "Tiger Feet", "48 Crash" – were, though utterly without the political agenda, as visceral and dynamic and razor-sharp as punk rock was later to be.

Abba understood that, and tried keenly to emulate the crispness of what became known as the "Chinnichap" sound. They couldn't quite capture it on the second album, and they can't quite capture it here. "Hey, Hey Helen" is just one of the tracks which shoots for the heart of glitter rock but hits it somewhere around the kneecaps.

Pounding drumbeat. Tasty guitar rifferama. So far, such a good intro. But the riff soon turns into a schoolboy AC/DC lick, starting to wheeze and plod. The vocals just refuse to fit (though the girls' falsetto backing is angelic – angelic but inappropriate). Then there's the would-be "funky" breakdown into a synth solo, a hint of Stevie Wonder's superior funk records of the time – "Superstition", "Higher Ground", etc. It's juicy, but again incongruous. Abba's own formula is just over the crest of the next hill…

This strange attempted fusion of glitter and funk seems to be telling the tale of Helen, "a woman of today" who's left her husband and kids to be "free at last". It skips every serious issue it can skip, but appears to be supportive of Helen. "Can you make it alone? Yes you can."

Tropical Loveland

When they miss the spot, Abba *really* miss it. "Tropical Loveland" is another of their cod-reggae confections, which makes you want to jump up and down and shout, "For God's sake, you're white, guys! You're one of the whitest bands who ever lived!" This kind of track has Ace Of Base to answer for, probably. And Peter Andre, for that matter. Its laughable attempts at "authentic" reggae tropes only exacerbate the irritation factor. Frida sings like a bored nun (er… without the seething levels of repressed passion that might imply) and there appears to be an accordion in there somewhere. Frida herself later called it "pretty uninteresting". Got that right, Fri.

Everything here smacks of "what we did on our holidays". Abba are forcing us to look at their vacation snapshots, one by one. "I wanna share it with you…" It's no surprise that Stig was involved in the composition of this one. "Life can be funny, happy and sunny/In my tropical loveland…" And moving on, with a brisk shake of the head…

"FRIDA HERSELF LATER CALLED IT 'PRETTY UNINTERESTING'."

S.O.S.

Just as it seemed Abba were doomed to be the "Waterloo" one hit wonders forever in Britain, this song – eighteen months down the line – saved them. It put them back in the top ten (top six, to be anal), and opened up chapter upon chapter. Most fans consider it their first truly transcendent classic, and certainly Agnetha – allowed to express some real personality for once – delivers a poignant, moving vocal. For many, although Frida came into her own, Agnetha's the star of this album. Michael Tretow once famously said she could "cry with her voice".

She revisited the song on her next solo album, but right here is where she starts crying. (On Hallstrom's film she stares forlornly at the camera. The boys added the famous guitar-and-synth motif, that makes the intro and drives the song, in the studio at the eleventh hour, in a late-night decision.

You almost want to give Agnetha, poor lamb, a hug as she pleads, "Whatever happened to our love? I wish I understood/It used to be so nice, it used to be good." Not for the only time, Bjorn's naïve use of English stumbles upon a highly emotive phrase. The production shows restraint, holding everything back for the big dips and surges when it counts. There's an unfortunate wibbly keyboard bloop, like something Rick Wakeman might have concocted, but the multi-tracked chorus, with acoustic guitars and more voices than you could shake a stick at, is glorious. It's a killer melody, of course, and there's aggression in the heartache. The final piano notes leave desire, regret and hope hanging in the air…

Agnetha may have been perceived as the sex symbol of Abba, but she was also during this period at least, the member most able to convey heartbreak. The boys may have been the boffins and musicians, and Frida may have been technically the more qualified chanteuse. But getting a pop song to hit the listener where they live is an indefinable art. Agnetha had a priceless gift for it.

Bjorn was immensely gratified when one of his idols approached him in New York. It was Pete Townshend of The Who, who expressed the opinion that "S.O.S." is one of the best pop songs ever written. Remember, he wasn't deaf back then. Few, to this day, would argue with the venerable rock legend.

Man In The Middle

From the sublime to the ridiculous, Abba kill the mood again with this galumphing attempt at "funkiness". Those Stevie Wonder-lite synths are in attendance again, and Bjorn's vocals are as vapid as ever (Michael Tretow gamely, if desperately, tried treating them with anything he could lay his hands on) until the girls come in to give him a lift. This was the last album to feature more than one lead vocal by Bjorn. Let us try, through politeness, to restrain our whoops of celebration. Though the guitars are slick, the "groove" resolutely refuses to take off. The words are interesting if slightly hypocritical. In a prelude to "Money Money Money", they chastise rich older men who cruise about in limousines wooing nubile teenagers and getting themselves "a belly full of lobster and caviar". These terrible, terrible men will apparently "drink champagne… while the rest of us drink beer". Evil incarnate! Hanging's too good for 'em, I say. Let us not be troubled here by the fact that Abba were very well off indeed at the time of their writing this song, and were soon to be rich enough to buy a country or five, should they so choose. It would be nice to think that they still drank beer.

Even Abba, after this, began to twig they couldn't "do" funk. It was a significant realisation, and perhaps we should be grateful for the woeful "Man In The Middle", because it drove them to strive to create "Dancing Queen".

> **"IT'S A KILLER MELODY, OF COURSE, AND THERE'S AGGRESSION IN THE HEARTACHE. THE FINAL PIANO NOTES LEAVE DESIRE, REGRET AND HOPE HANGING IN THE AIR…"**

Bang-A-Boomerang

A song that Abba believed in, to little avail. They'd recorded it before, then dismissed it, then rewritten large sections of it. Then Bjorn and Benny (and Stig) gave it to Polar wannabes Svenne & Lotta to perform at the Eurovision heats in Sweden. Could Svenne & Lotta follow in the famous footsteps of Abba with an Abba song? Um, no. In fact, they only came third among the Swedish entries.

Bjorn and Benny were worried that the song was now tarnished as a loser. Then again, they were thrifty, practical chaps. They overdubbed Abba vocals onto the pre-recorded backing track, sure the song could be a hit somewhere. It was a hit nowhere.

Would the world be a lesser place without the following? "Like a bang, a boom-a-boomerang/ Dum de dum dum, be dum be dum/ Oh bang, bang a boomerang/ Love is a tune you hum de hum hum".

Its shuffling, peripatetic drumbeat pushes along a blatantly Spector-esque, Beach Boys-influenced, Eurovision banker (you'd think). The girls' voices – which go higher and higher and higher – are compressed in a manner reminiscent of "Mamma Mia". The lyrics are inane (although the "na na na" bit works efficiently) and the chords and chorus are brash and unsubtle. "Bang-A-Boomerang" is trying too hard. The bridge leaving the verse sounds forced and contrived, and the phrase Eurovision Also Ran is stamped on its forehead. Interestingly, Eurovision 1975 was won by a (Dutch) song called – wait for it – "Ding Ding A Dong". Sheesh, it's like "Waterloo" never happened...

I Do, I Do, I Do, I Do, I Do

It was supposed to be the song to re-establish Abba in Britain. Despite a panicky, desperate promo campaign by the record company, who saw this single as the launch-pad for the album, the British didn't want anything to do with it. Unless you count getting to number 38 something to do with it. *Melody Maker* called the song: "so bad it hurts". The Australians, however, utterly loved it, and went slightly overboard, even later sending its b-side ("Rock Me") into the top five.

> **"ITS MELODY IS AS HUGE AS A BATTLESHIP, AND BOY DO ABBA KNOW IT, PRODUCING IT TO WITHIN AN INCH OF ITS LIFE."**

The song was inspired by Bjorn and Benny's music heritage, and their love of Fifties saxophone orchestras, especially the one led by Billy Vaughan in the States. All in all, "I Do...", a ballroom dance blitz, is as odd and wonderful and tasteless as its title. It's a bit camp, a bit vaudeville, a bit cabaret. Its melody is as huge as a battleship, and boy do Abba know it, producing it to within an inch of its life. The screeching, in-your-face wall of sound threatens to crush both the song, and you. The bells give it a festive feel; the saxes are somehow

both raunchy and nostalgic. "I Do…" doesn't so much have a chorus as *is* one big chorus. Now *here's* a song which has graced a wedding or two, and not just in popular Australian romantic comedies starring Toni Collette…

When it comes to this song - outside Australia, almost a pop-trivia test question in itself (if Abba, in trying to write a hit, penned a complete bomb, how would it sound?) – you either love it or you don't, you don't, you don't, you don't, you don't.

Rock Me

Wooaaarrgghh! Rise up kerrang-ing spawn of hell and storm the celestial barricades: Bjorn is rocking. Bjorn, in fact, is rock. Or, at least, that's how it probably sounded in his head. "Rock Me" is

silly, embarrassing, and, like most things Abba, terrific fun. In its own bonkers way, it kind of works.

Wishing it was heavy metal but much closer to that period Chinnichap/glitter sound as epitomised by The Rubettes, Arrows and Kenny (and the drumbeat nods to Motown), "Rock Me" was a b-side which turned a-side in Oz. With its tacky power chords and attempted raciness (substitute a certain f-word for "rock" throughout the song and it makes more rather than less sense), it's nothing if not energetic. Abba pull off that trick of everyone dropping out then piling back in again so well, and there's a slight hello to Limmie and the Family Cookin's pop nugget "You Can Do Magic".

The talking point here, though, is Bjorn's vocal. So many times, up to this point, his reedy pipes have allowed an otherwise perky song to die on its arse. We've consistently wondered why the boys don't just check in their egos at the studio door and let Agnetha and Frida tackle all the vocals. But here, he has personality. Let's not get carried away: it's not as if he sings *well*, or anything. But he does sing with a gravelly macho gusto which is scorched and sandpapered. He's evidently been listening a lot to Noddy Holder of Slade.

> **"SO MANY TIMES, UP TO THIS POINT, HIS REEDY PIPES HAVE ALLOWED AN OTHERWISE PERKY SONG TO DIE ON ITS ARSE."**

The song became something of an Abba live favourite. Well, either that or Bjorn sulked and insisted he got to do his strutting about being a rock god bit every night. I mean, it wasn't as if the audience primarily came to look at the girls. Was it?

Intermezzo No. 1

What a contrast! Benny's spotlight moment is this quasi-classical instrumental, a gigantic swirling slab of pomp rock which few, other than aficionados, would ever recognise as Abba. Mike Oldfield's epochal *Tubular Bells* was big at the time, and Queen were getting very cod-operatic. This dry ice anthem appears to Benny's stab at a "Fanfare For The Common Man" (as popularised by Emerson, Lake & Palmer), where he shows off his keyboard and arranging skills, presumably while wearing a silky cape and lots of spandex. Somewhere between the kind of music Ken Russell would love and the theme to a televised motor racing event, it starts with aplomb but, like most pomp rock gets wearing quite quickly.

Still, if Bjorn was allowed to rock out, Benny was certainly permitted to do his ersatz extracts from *Fantasia*. Originally entitled "Mama", it too was a live fave – either that or Benny insisted he got to do his Rick Wakeman bit every night…

One imagines him noodling away on his banks of synths like a mad professor, on a revolving plinth, creating the missing link between *Spinal Tap* and The Last Night Of The Proms.

It was the penultimate instrumental ever to appear on an Abba album.

I've Been Waiting For You

Not to be confused with the classic Neil Young song recently covered by David Bowie, this lush, multi-layered ballad brought the album back to sanity, with Agnetha hitting all the right heartbreak buttons. Her voice has a way here of just skirting the edges of the melody, as if through the sheer force of emotion she.s being pushed to the very edge… yet hanging on.

The intro threatens to turn a touch Celine Dion, but the song settles in smoothly with what sound like a thousand multi-tracked acoustic guitars.

Agnetha's voice spirals ever higher, and the "na na na" section is very affecting. There's sweet lead guitar work, nicely judged and never over the top. Subtle and warm – just when the album seemed to veering towards the histrionic – "I've Been Waiting For You" is big without being bombastic. Abba were moving closer to producing a perfect ballad.

So Long

"You think you're gonna make me softer, with your fancy car/ But I can tell you that your tricks ain't gonna get you far…" Another blast of sheer pop energy which tumbles over itself in its desire to please. It's easy with hindsight to see why "So Long" missed out as an intended hit (it even

flopped in Sweden) – it's just too eager, too hurried, grinning and rubbing itself up against your leg, all idea of mystery and seduction readily sacrificed. The shrill guitar intro sets the tone (Benny and Bjorn had reservations about the way the track was recorded), then with a nod to 10CC's "Rubber

Bullets" we get a surge of updated rock'n'roll; Chuck Berry gone Glitter. There's a stonking chorus (of course), and the girls' voices sound like they're on helium or speed. Next to this even Mud's "The Cat Crept In" sounded like a shy, sly tease. "Tracy, Daisy, they may be crazy/ But I'll never be your

"IT'S EASY WITH HINDSIGHT TO SEE WHY *SO LONG* MISSED OUT AS AN INTENDED HIT (IT EVEN FLOPPED IN SWEDEN) – IT'S JUST TOO EAGER, TOO HURRIED."

girl…" The piano fills over the fade are very Mud, very Chinnichap. Melody is lost in the headlong rush. Exciting, yes. But exhausting too.

"So Long" made little impact in the U.K, where it can't be over-stressed that "S.O.S." and "Mamma Mia" saved their career. The *ABBA* album reaped the dividends claimed by those two songs. Abba were no longer one-hit wonders, but neither were they yet household names. That was just around the corner. Now they really *were* about to go supernova…

BONUS TRACKS on 2001 reissue:
Crazy World

Another Bjorn lead vocal, it was left off the original album at the last minute. Reworked, it made the b-side of the "Money, Money, Money" single in late '76. A tad twee, it's instrumentally evocative of Demis Roussos records being played by an overzealous hostess in Mike Leigh's *Abigail's Party*. Once again it proves Abba considered no genre to be beyond or above, or indeed beneath, them. The lyric's especially corny in the story-telling mode then being used more successfully by the likes of Bobby Goldsboro, Lobo and Albert

Hammond, Bjorn getting jealous of a man he spies emerging from his lover's house. Turns out it's her brother. What a cunning twist! The relief prompts Bjorn to sigh: "It's a crazy world". So very true.

Medley: Pick A Bale Of Cotton/On Top of Old Smokey/ Midnight Special

"Traditional" folk songs, vamped up by the Swedes after watching too many episodes of *The Waltons*. It's all very slap-your-thighs-around-the-campfire, while wearing dodgy checked flannel shirts and dungarees and chewing on a straw. The frenetic drummer expresses a wish to be Animal from *The Muppets*. The girls' vocals sound weirdly disembodied, and the whole thing's funnier than intended. Whose idea was this? Obviously a result of their still touring the Swedish folk parks throughout summer '75, it was recorded in May of that year for a cancer charity album. It's the only non-band composition ever released by Abba, and re-emerged on the flipside of the 1978 single "Summer Night City".

ARRIVAL 1976

Recorded August 1975 - September 1976 at Metronome and Glen Studios, Stockholm.

Produced by Benny Andersson and Bjorn Ulvaeus. Engineered by Michael Tretow.

Musicians: Bjorn Ulvaeus (acoustic and electric guitars), Benny Andersson (keyboards, synthesisers, marimbas, chimes, accordions, pianos), Rutger Gunnarson (bass, string arrangements), Ola Brunkert (drums), Roger Palm (drums on "Dancing Queen"), Malando Gassama (percussion), Janne Schaffer (guitar), Anders Glenmark (guitar), Lasse Wellander (guitar), AndersDahl (string arrangements), Sven-Olof Walldoff (violin arrangements), Lasse Carlsson (sax).

Vocals by Abba. (Solo vocals by Agnetha ("My Love, My Life", "When I Kissed The Teacher"), Frida ("Knowing Me, Knowing You", "Money, Money, Money"), Bjorn ("Why Did It Have To Be Me?").

WHEN I KISSED THE TEACHER

DANCING QUEEN

MY LOVE, MY LIFE

DUM DUM DIDDLE

KNOWING ME, KNOWING YOU

MONEY, MONEY, MONEY

THAT'S ME

WHY DID IT HAVE TO BE ME?

TIGER

ARRIVAL

Bonus Tracks on 2001 Reissue:

FERNANDO

HAPPY HAWAII

THEY ARRIVED, ALL RIGHT. THIS WAS THE ALBUM THAT MADE ABBA, THAT ELEVATED THEM TO THE STATUS OF GLOBALLY REVERED, ICONIC POP DEITIES. OR PERHAPS WE SHOULD SAY THESE WERE THE *SONGS* WHICH MADE ABBA, FOR SINGLES LIKE "DANCING QUEEN", "KNOWING ME, KNOWING YOU" AND "MONEY, MONEY, MONEY" WOWED THE WORLD AND PROVED THAT ABBA WEREN'T GOING TO LET THE HOLY GRAIL SLIP AWAY THIS TIME.

Their music reached a new level of maturity and their image was slicker and more self-assured. Abba were hitting their peak. By August '77, the rarely shy Stig Anderson was able to announce to the world's media that Abba had sold fifty million records worldwide: thirty million albums and twenty million singles. The press lapped it up, proclaiming that Abba were now "bigger than The Beatles".

The hard work had paid off – 1975 had been absurdly busy for the foursome, and the *Arrival* album took over a year to complete. As well as touring, they'd been undergoing endless television promotional work all over the planet. Benny was producing Frida's Swedish language solo opus, while Agnetha too was putting together another album. It wasn't long before the twin commitments

motherhood and the Abba schedule proved too unforgiving for Agnetha, and the solo career was, with realistically a sense of relief, put on hold. With Australia clamouring, and "Mamma Mia" and "SOS" hits everywhere, Abba had little or no time to concentrate on writing new songs.

One they did come up with – "Fernando" – was rush-released as a new single. It had been conceived as a track for Frida's album, and been a Swedish hit for her, but the need for a new Abba single and their realisation that it was a winner meant that the plan was re-jigged. "Fernando" did more than buy them time. In Australia it held the top spot for fourteen weeks, equalling The Beatles' all-time record, set with "Hey Jude". An Abba TV special in Australia also broke all records for viewing figures. More people there watched it onscreen than had watched the 1969 Apollo moon landing.

Many factors came together to make *Arrival* the crucial Abba album to date. Disco was emerging, and Abba produced their own distinctive take on that. They were beginning to realise the strengths of using the girls' voices, together and separately, more prominently than the men's, and at the same time Bjorn and Benny's songwriting was moving into its greatest ever period.

With the huge success of "Fernando" (a number one in Britain too), audiences had accepted that the band weren't mere Eurovision novelty fodder. The sheer quality of the next three singles – "Dancing Queen", "Money, Money, Money" and "Knowing Me, Knowing You" – did the rest. Abba-mania snowballed. *Arrival* sold bucket loads; the back catalogue sales benefited as a spin-off. Even Bjorn and Benny, who'd had misguidedly repeated their wish for Abba to be perceived as an albums

band and not a singles band like a mantra, must surely have been satisfied now.

Of course, life doesn't work out so neatly. At a time when they should have been at their happiest, the two Abba couples were stressed and strained, experiencing relationship troubles. Which made for some vastly improved lyrics, at least. Being true professionals, they didn't allow any arguments or grief to show onscreen or onstage. The world still thought of Abba as two cuddly shiny couples.

" *GREATEST HITS..* STAYED IN THE CHARTS FOR AN ASTONISHING 130 WEEKS AS ABBA FEVER EXPLODED. "

As if all this wasn't enough, in March '76 Abba had cunningly released *Greatest Hits* (later referred to as *Greatest Hits Volume 1*). Giving them more than a hint that the world was primed and moist for *Arrival*, it rocketed to number one in the U.K. (their first album chart topper there), and, featuring "Fernando", stayed in the charts for an astonishing 130 weeks as Abba fever exploded. In November, *Arrival* of course claimed the top spot, residing on the chart for a massive 92 weeks. Abba were to enjoy seven more number one albums in Britain.

They were the biggest-selling act in both singles and albums charts for 1976, *Greatest Hits* being the year's undisputed champ. (Only a Beach Boys compilation, Demis Roussos and Wings came anywhere close). Singles-wise, the ghost of Eurovision came back to haunt them, as Brotherhood Of Man's "Save Your Kisses For Me" nabbed the top-selling single spot for the year, closely followed by Elton John and Kiki Dee with "Don't Go Breaking My Heart". "Dancing Queen" (over half a million sales) showed at number four, "Fernando" at seven. ("Knowing Me, Knowing You" was released in 1977, a year in which *Arrival* was the biggest-selling album by a mile.)

These were mere details: Abba were obscenely big in Australia and most other places, and "Dancing Queen" finally cracked America for them, making number one there. They were compared to The Mamas and the Papas.

Even the British music press, notoriously enraged by commercial success, warmed to *Arrival*. "Abba are irrepressible", said the *NME*. "Their songs are structured as surely as a Timex. They might be dismantled but would only function if put back together in the same way...They deliver their material with such gusto that, if you try to turn a deaf ear, they'll just pummel your brain into submission." The *NME* went on to analyse ticket demand for the group's shows, and proved that Abba could fill the Royal Albert Hall 624 times over.

Touring continued apace, with the live shows and sets getting increasingly exotic and expensive, but Abba knew they were really famous when bizarre rumours began to circulate that they'd died in a tragic plane crash. These were then modified: three members had died but Frida had survived –

however she was so appallingly injured that she'd never sing again. Emanating from Germany, these rumours enraged Abba and their management, and Bjorn had to make a special appearance on German television to put them to rest.

Arrival is the Abba of legend, the Abba who had their finger on the pulse of that thing we call "perfect pop". In this case, the over-used, clichéd phrase was justified and entirely accurate. There were fewer silly "wacky" lyrics, there was less lapsing into the "schlager" aesthetic. (Only "Dum Dum

Diddle" really let the side down.) Agnetha and Frida were more involved than ever, as was unsung hero Michael Tretow. Bjorn and Frida had turned thirty and Benny was about to. Abba were grown-ups.

Arrival is testament to Abba's sophisticated, sincere vision of how panoramic pop can be. It's as serious as the wilfully lightweight ever gets. Any music-lover who doesn't feel a rush of electricity through their veins every time the supercharged intro to "Dancing Queen" kicks in, or doesn't experience a pang in the heart at the beginning of the sublime melancholy that is "Knowing Me, Knowing You", is not a music-lover.

All Alan Partridge jokes aside. A-ha!

When I Kissed The Teacher

One of Bjorn's favourite Abba tracks, which proves once again that he was a very strange man. A curious choice for an album opener, it begins in a hazy swirl of effects, the spectre of Spector still dominating Abba's decisions. Agnetha's solo vocal remains oddly hazy and spooky, even when the drums kick in. Eventually, she's allowed to stride forth, the high backing vocals get intricate, and the number comes to life... sort of. Uncharacteristically sloppy rhythms don't help.

The Fifties-ish lyrics concern a schoolgirl who has a crush on her teacher. To the alarm of the class, she then actually – gasp – kisses him, the naughty Lolita. Whether Sting was inspired thus to write The Police's hit "Don't Stand So Close To Me" is unconfirmed. The teacher in the Abba song is

"trying to explain the laws of geometry". So it's understandable that bored young pupils' minds would turn to steamier affairs. Our girl vows she's "gonna teach him a lesson alright". The little minx.

Ultimately, "When I Kissed The Teacher" doesn't sound like the innocent, impish fun you expect from its title and theme. It sounds like something that wishes it was celestial. Except with slack drumming. It ain't got that swing. The next track, however, has it like few others have ever had it...

Dancing Queen

It's the ultimate party record, the one which not so much breaks as stomps on then melts the ice at every drunken office celebration. Karaoke probably wouldn't exist without it, and 87% of all British married couples wouldn't be together without its intoxicating effects. Okay, there's possibly some exaggeration in that last figure, but there's no denying the all-pervading, inhibition-conquering, *joie-de-vivre*-gushing euphoria of this dancefloor monster, somehow both the greatest disco hit of all time and yet not remotely disco at all. Abba always got things (genres, styles) just a little bit askew, and that accidental left-handed charm is a huge factor in what makes them so magical to our ears.

Having consolidated on their breakthrough successes with "Fernando", Abba needed to either ride the booming disco wave or circumnavigate it. They did both: "Dancing Queen" hints vaguely at disco rhythms like those popularised by producers Casey (aka KC) & Finch on George McRae's seminal "Rock Your Baby" or KC & The Sunshine Band's "Queen Of Clubs", but is melodically so strong that it transcends mere genre. Though based around simple chords (the famous and arresting intro is nothing more ambitious or "difficult" than a switch between A and D: trust me, that's pretty basic), the song just keeps swirling and spiralling higher and higher until even the most curmudgeonly grump is coerced into falsetto-ing along. Not to mention waving their hands in the air like they just don't care. It's often referred to as a gay anthem, but frankly it's just very happy.

Early Abba's gauche yet winning way with words can be spotted again here. Apparently, not only can you dance, but you can "jive", as you're "diggin'" the dancing queen. And though they gamely try to walk and talk this new-fangled thing called disco, the Swedish ex-folkies rather blow their cover by proclaiming that "with a bit of rock music, everything is fine". Still, this has all given Abba an added so-naff-it's-cool camp value over the years. Which other band, in attempting to stoke up a little Friday Night Fever, would urge you to "feel the beat from the tambourine"?

Whatever – it swept away everything in its path, and still does every time it comes on in your favourite sweaty after-hours party place. A British number one, of course, and the group's only American chart-topper. "Dancing Queen" bestrides the landscape of Seventies pop like a badly dressed but agile, sensitive and very handsome giant.

That piano-and-guitar intro technique of Bjorn and Benny's hits its zenith here (Elvis Costello rather pilfered it for "Oliver's Army" and is still quoting and referencing this song on his own albums to this day.) Even Benny's frilly jangling can't scupper the irresistible momentum, and the girls' voices work together like a well-oiled machine. Every ingredient contributes magically to the whole… even those subtle little rhythmic skips after each chorus.

Is this Abba's finest moment? Benny's said as much. Frida certainly thought so. She burst into tears when she first heard the soaring backing track. It'd begun to come together under the working title of "Boogaloo", but shifted gradually as the Swedes took on board the grooves of George McRae and even, drummer Roger Palm has said, Dr. John. There were rumours that Abba had written the new lyric for the King of Sweden's new bride. Bunkum, of course, but they (and, naturally, Stig) let the story breathe as it didn't do them any harm in their homeland. Queen Silvia may have been "young and sweet", but she certainly wasn't "only seventeen". She was only thirty-something.

"Dancing Queen" has been number one in more countries than it hasn't. It enjoyed six weeks at the top in Britain through September and October, eventually giving way to Pussycat's "Mississippi". Which has proven slightly less durable.

> **"DANCING QUEEN BESTRIDES THE LANDSCAPE OF SEVENTIES POP LIKE A BADLY DRESSED BUT AGILE, SENSITIVE AND VERY HANDSOME GIANT."**

My Love, My Life

Abba again demonstrate their customary disregard for anything resembling an album flow or a track order that makes sonic sense of any kind. Having got us on our feet, they dizzyingly change the mood with a deathly slow ballad, although admittedly *anything* would be an anticlimax after "Dancing Queen". On its own terms, this Agnetha-sung misery-fest is sweet enough, though eventually more yawn-making than tear-jerking. The interplay between the voices on the chorus is delightful. It may resemble most closely, among other Abba numbers, "Fernando" or "Chiquitita", but it's draggy and dreary.

> "IT MAY RESEMBLE MOST CLOSELY, AMONG OTHER ABBA NUMBERS, *FERNANDO* OR *CHIQUITITA*, BUT IT'S DRAGGY AND DREARY."

What sets it apart is Agnetha's intoxicating sibilance when pronouncing the letter "s", and the semi-broken English evident when she speaks the line, "Tell me, is it really so hard to say?" The emotion she pours into the closing, "you're still my one and only" is convincing too. The kind of song that makes people wonder what was going on (or wrong) at this time in Agnetha's marriage to Bjorn.

It was one of the last tracks on the album to be completed, and had begun life as a quirkier, more upbeat ditty called "Monsieur, Monsieur", but seemed to fit snugly into a more leisurely style of arrangement. When Bjorn and Benny heard 10CC's international chart-topper "I'm Not In Love", they decided to emulate its use of massed, treated vocals as an ambient texture. In a very Abba kind of way, the result was a tiny fraction askew.

Dum Dum Diddle

Would they ever learn? The puerile wackiness is back on this silly confection, coloured by Swedish folk fiddle music, which Frida rightly proclaimed: "A silly song – I do not like it." At least they're not apes sitting in a tree eulogising astronauts this time, but… actually, it's worse. Our pitiable narrator falls in love with a violinist, and wishes she could become his "darling" fiddle - "to be so near you and not just hear you". For some reason, ghastly visions of Charles and Camilla are starting to come into my mind…

Many's the song that's begged you play the singer's heart like you play your old guitar, but this is just daft. Worse, the fiddles don't even sound like fiddles – they're a horrible, synthesised contrivance.

Years on, Bjorn confessed he'd scrawled the strained lyrics just before dawn in an exhausted fit of desperation. It shows. Sometimes the Abba hit-writing factory had exemplary quality control. Other times, well…

From the ridiculous to the sublime…

Knowing Me,
Knowing You

Cast from your mind Steve Coogan's bubble-bursting satirical sketches and this still stands up as one of the most majestic, moving pop songs of all time. Who can fail to be floored by that ominous, overwrought intro? By Frida's deep, dramatic vocal? By the warbling synths which flesh out the stark piano/guitar stabs? And by that awesome, brooding, building melody, by those heartbroken yet resilient lyrics? This is where Abba well and truly grew up.

Bjorn's story of a dying romance "no more care-free laughter, silence ever after…" may have been painfully close to home, but it sure made for a better, more durable song than Stig's usual happy-happy-holidays lyrical contributions. (Stig had, in fairness, suggested the title. But it was Bjorn who'd taken the idea and run to previously unexplored recesses with it). Abba were suddenly singing to millions of their lives behind closed doors. When Agnetha joins Frida a little way into the song, the two are at their telepathic best, the stunning backing vocals arrangements as intricate as a stained glass window. And Bjorn's even allowed a proper guitar sound for once…

He's often denied that the song was about his own troubled marriage. It's "ninety per cent fiction", he's said, adding that he hadn't yet been through such a situation – divorce – himself. He's admitted though that the song's "roots" were from "somewhere deep inside". It's been documented that Agnetha was keener on motherhood than promoting

Abba, while Bjorn was more into band-related activities than domestic bliss. The couple had always been volatile. Agnetha had described her husband as a "workaholic". She was tiring of travelling; he was aware he'd regret it forever if he didn't capitalise on this spreading success. The marriage was under enormous, spotlit pressure.

The whispered call-and-response ("memories", "always") is another titanic set piece. "Knowing Me, Knowing You" is "Seven Rooms Of Gloom" meets "By The Time I Get To Phoenix", both grandiose and intimate. A sexy, sad, suspenseful record, it's the moment where Abba stake their claim for immortality.

That surging "a-haaa" has much to answer for, but is surely among pop's most memorable, treasurable tropes.

The first track to be recorded for *Arrival*, the song displaced Manhattan Transfer's "Chanson D'Amour" (which itself echoed, for better or worse, "I Do, I Do, I Do, I Do, I Do") from number one in the UK in April '77. It spent five weeks at the top, finally being toppled by Deneice Williams' "Free". (Was this really the year of punk rock??) It was the year's fifth biggest seller. (Hardened, mohican-sporting anti-Christ David Soul's "Don't Give Up On Us" came first.)

Oddly, it was one of their lesser hits in Australia, scraping to number nine, but then the ebbs and flows of Abba's career there always defied reason. "Knowing Me, Knowing You" remains a stone classic.

> " AGNETHA HAD DESCRIBED HER HUSBAND AS A 'WORKAHOLIC'. "

Money, Money, Money

Though it peaked at number three in Britain over Christmas 1976, and was rejected as a single for the American market, "Money, Money, Money" retains a prized, precious place in the Abba pantheon. A terrific showcase for Frida's range and sense of humour, it was almost rewritten by Bjorn, who though the theme – money's the root of all evil – had been used too often by others (and indeed by Abba, on "Man In The Middle"). He considered re-titling it "Gypsy Girl". Everyone agreed the song worked much better as "Money, Money, Money", however, and so another Australian – and German, Dutch, Belgian, New Zealand and Mexican – number one single was born.

It allowed Abba to play around with their image, too. For Lasse Hallstrom's video, Agnetha and Frida looked stunning and decidedly strange in jazz age flapper dresses and pearls, feathers in their hair. The song owed a huge debt to Bob Fosse's movie *Cabaret*, which starred Liza (with a "zee") Minelli as be-stockinged Berlin nightclub chanteuse Sally Bowles. "Money makes the world go around", that film had opined. Here, Frida groaned that she was working all night and day to pay the bills, but still was broke. Her plan, she confessed, was to nab a wealthy man. "All the things I could do, if I had a little money, in a rich man's world". Although, comes the surprise quip, "If he happens to be free, I bet he wouldn't fancy me…" She concludes by vowing to win a fortune in Vegas or Monaco.

The track is exquisitely arranged (verse and chorus are wildly contrasting). It hints at Benny and Bjorn's ambitions towards stage musicals, which

were to be further explored on the next album. Benny's keyboards are insanely flamboyant and there's an ending straight out of the old MGM Fred Astaire/Ginger Rogers movies. There's even another "a-haaa" sneaked in…

Notwithstanding his love of "Dancing Queen", Benny has expressed a hunch that this is his favourite Abba track. (God knows he expresses himself enough on it). He likes the way it's "constructed like a stage number". Rows were frequent in the studio at this time, and Frida's all-guns-blazing delivery may have been precipitated by some inter-personal stroppiness.

The huge irony of a group of millionaires – challenging Volvo as Sweden's most lucrative export – bemoaning a lack of cash was, they've claimed, intentional. They were taking the Mick out of themselves. Well, they would have to say that, wouldn't they? "Money, Money, Money" helped to make plenty more of the stuff. Must be funny.

> **"NOTWITHSTANDING HIS LOVE OF *DANCING QUEEN*, BENNY HAS EXPRESSED A HUNCH THAT THIS IS HIS FAVOURITE ABBA TRACK."**

That's Me

D-I-S-C-O! Abba try to get with the rhythms of the times and do the hustle, the shuffle, and anything else you may have seen/heard in a Seventies movie based on a Jackie Collins novel and starring her sister Joan. Not quite managing to match the Bee Gees' contributions to *Saturday Night Fever*, Abba confirm that "Dancing Queen" was special. Everything fell together there. Here, it doesn't. Not that the track's a turkey – it lollops along comfortably enough, suggesting that a blue-print for such subsequent gems as "Gimme Gimme Gimme" and "Voulez Vous" was being sketched out. Those swooping and soaring keyboard lines needed trimming though, Benny.

And what a weird, faintly creepy lyric this is. Probably inspired by the Brian De Palma horror flick *Carrie*, it has a girl telling a suitor that she's "an angel in disguise" and "not a man's toy": by her own admission she's a fiery, high-maintenance sort to get involved with. "I'm Carrie, not the kind of girl you'd marry… I don't believe in fairy tales, sweet nothings in my ear…" Not exactly "let's all boogie", is it?

In an alternate universe somewhere, this was chosen as a single instead of "Dancing Queen" and Abba are now working in a burger bar.

Why Did It Have To Be Me?

And why *does* it have to be you, Bjornykins? Tea break everyone, Bjorn's singing. The girls mercifully relieve him (and us) after a minute or so, thankfully. A plodding-through-cement piano-led singalong, this – the very last track to be recorded for *Arrival* – is Abba doing Chas'n'Dave doing Denis Waterman, and every bit as inelegant and hobnail-booted as that sounds. If you were bending over backwards to be kind, you could say it was a tribute to the Seventies hits of Gilbert O'Sullivan and Hurricane Smith. Or even that it was a shot at emulating Fats Domino. That would be generous. It's hard – nay, impossible – to believe that the same outfit could produce such flights of genius as "Dancing Queen" and "Knowing Me…" on the same album as this.

The saxes struggle to escape back to the relative quality of "I Do, I Do, I Do, I Do, I Do", the melody's hammered home with a mallet. Only the split-second where the girls gasp, "I only wanted a little love affair" reveals any class or pop sensibility (Frida bailed Bjorn out by duetting this song live). You can take the gang out of Eurovision, but you can't completely take the Eurovision out of the gang…

As if this wasn't enough of a duffer, wait till you hear about "Happy Hawaii"… to all intents and purposes, the same song. Stay with us, masochists.

Tiger

Frida and Agnetha are at their combined, feline best on this surprisingly rocky number. It became a firm crowd favourite as the set-opener (following loud, helicopter sound effects) on Abba's phenomenally successful tours of this period.

A kind of elder, more reserved brother to Survivor's "Eye Of The Tiger" *Rocky* theme song, it finds Abba wandering the mean streets – "the city is a jungle". But they are to be feared, not the urban sprawl: "I am behind you, I will always find you, I am the tiger." One's never quite sure why Agnetha and Frida aren't a "tigress", and the line "If I meet you, what if I eat you?" is either very risqué or very naïve (almost certainly the latter). But better we have mucky lyrics than wacky ones. The drums swagger with panache, the guitar sound's halfway aggressive (rare for Abba) and the clever bridge, well, rocks. The flourish with which the girls execute the final three yells of "Tiger!" is genuinely thrilling.

"YOU CAN TAKE THE GANG OUT OF EUROVISION, BUT YOU CAN'T COMPLETELY TAKE THE EUROVISION OUT OF THE GANG…"

Arrival

An instrumental – the album title came first – which requires a tolerance for bagpipe sounds. I have none, and so find this a cross between an Edinburgh Tattoo military march and "Auld Lang Syne". Mike Oldfield later elected to cover it, presumably thinking its composers could

BONUS TRACKS on 2001 reissue:
Fernando

Having featured in Swedish on a Frida solo album (alongside, incidentally, her cover of 10CC's "The Wall Street Shuffle" – she had a thing about money), the Abba *Greatest Hits* collection, and as a massive single all over the world, Fernando was considered superfluous when *Arrival* was first released. A phenomenon in Australia, it had topped the UK charts for four weeks in May '76, in between – here's quality – The Brotherhood Of Man and the Wurzels. It had been ready to release at the same time as "Dancing Queen" – Stig, cleverly, thought they could gamble on following "Mamma Mia" with a slow ballad, and broadening their fan base, as "Dancing Queen" was a guaranteed smash anyway.

When it came to transforming Stig's mediocre Swedish lyrics (girl-loves-Fernando) to something more captivating for the English language market, Bjorn was again inspired. We're never quite sure which war is being sung about or why, but Bjorn's vision was of a pair of former revolutionaries, in Mexico, reminiscing over their wild fearless youth. They could still "hear the drums".

"Fernando", which sounded twee on release, has grown in stature since. The arrangement is delightful, and the chorus sweeps all before it. It's hardly the most gritty, authentic song ever written about freedom fighters, but its unspecific air and vagueness leaves enough gaps for the listener to fill in with their own fantasies/memories. There's a real sense of yearning, pride and regret.

Abba copyists The Brotherhood Of Man – and not for the only time – cobbled together their own

do with a few bob. Benny Beethoven may have been indulging a delusion of grandeur or two hereabouts, as he had on "Intermezzo No. 1". He was deeply fond of his Swedish folkie roots and even considered naming the track "Ode To Dalecarlia", Dalecarlia being a Swedish county known as a stronghold of folk music. This was the last time an instrumental featured on an Abba album. It's been revealed that, despite Abba's success, Frida was suffering from depression at the time of the *Arrival* album's recording and release. Maybe she'd had to listen to Benny writing and rehearsing this.

chart-topping rip-off, "Angelo" almost immediately. Abba had posterity to look forward to, however. Their stars were bright.

Happy Hawaii

Not a classic. Another of those occasions where Abba exhort everybody to pack up their troubles and enjoy a jolly holiday, and end up sounding about as transcendent as Boney M. Such songs were in vogue then, and perhaps always will be in the summer months. Less forgivably, this is "Why Did It Have To Be Me?" in different (gawdy) clothes. Bjorn had dabbled with the tune in various forms and styles (can't knock him for trying), and allowed Agnetha and Frida the vocal duties for this particularly perky one. It was eventually stashed away on the b-side of "Knowing Me, Knowing You".

Even Ulvaeus and Andersson recognised the excruciating naffness of the lyrics, and Bjorn later conceded, "the lyrics were just too damned corny". Rest assured, "sun" was rhymed with "fun".

THE ALBUM 1977

Recorded May - November 1977 at Marcus, Metronome and Glen Studios, Stockholm, and Bohus Studio, Kungalv.

Produced and arranged by Benny Andersson and Bjorn Ulvaeus. Engineered by Michael B. Tretow.

Musicians: Benny Andersson (all keyboards), Bjorn Ulvaeus (guitars), Rutger Gunnarsson (bass, string arrangements), Ola Brunkert (drums), Roger Palm (drums), Lasse Wellander (lead guitar), Janne Schaffer (lead guitar), Malando Gassama (percussion), Lars O. Carlsson (saxophone, flute).

Vocals by Abba.

EAGLE

TAKE A CHANCE ON ME

ONE MAN, ONE WOMAN

THE NAME OF THE GAME

MOVE ON

HOLE IN YOUR SOUL

THE GIRL WITH THE GOLDEN HAIR:
3 SCENES FROM A MINI-MUSICAL:
1 THANK YOU FOR THE MUSIC
2 I WONDER (DEPARTURE)
3 I'M A MARIONETTE

Bonus track on 2001 Reissue:

THANK YOU FOR THE MUSIC (DORIS DAY VERSION)

This was the (imaginatively titled) album wherein Abba made a concerted effort to tailor their sound to the American market, revealed their desire to write musicals, kept up their prolific work rate despite shooting a movie and Agnetha's being pregnant, and still remained unconscionably successful.

Stig and the band thought they'd dreamed up the perfect strategy for total world domination: *Abba – The Movie* and *Abba – The Album* were both to flood the pre-Christmas market. As it turned out, the group were to a small degree victims of their own success: pressing plants couldn't cope with the demand for the album in time, and in many areas it had to wait until the new year to hit the shops. Nevertheless, it did, as hoped, do well in the States over the course of 1978. "Take A Chance On Me" (yet another British number one – the seventh biggest seller of '78) reached the top three there, and eventually outsold "Dancing Queen", becoming Abba's best selling U.S. single. Inexplicably, their star was waning in Australia now – some blamed over-exposure, others blamed a few quiet months between singles. Nobody, not even Abba, had a magic wand.

Abba - The Album bore more of a clearly American influence than any of its predecessors. (At least, until the closing sections). Bjorn, Benny and Michael Tretow,

as part of their plan to build a state-of-the-art studio in Stockholm, had been scouting equipment in LA, and immersed themselves in the popular West Coast sounds of the era – The Eagles, Fleetwood Mac, and other radio-friendly soft-rockers.

"The Name Of The Game" was the first sign of their new, relatively progressive, less in-your-face direction. Preceding the album, it was welcomed and embraced by fans. It sauntered to number one in

Britain in November '77, staying there for four weeks between Baccara's (very Abba-esque) "Yes Sir, I Can Boogie" and Wings' all-conquering "Mull Of Kintyre". In the end-of-year lists it made number seventeen, although *Arrival* was '77's best-selling album (so much, again, for punk) and *Greatest Hits* came ninth. *Abba – The Album* was to prove the third biggest shifter of '78, beaten only by the phenomena of *Saturday Night Fever* and *Grease*. It spent a staggering sixty-one weeks on the chart, including seven at the summit.

Another innovation made by the record was its inclusion as a climax of a "mini-musical". Bjorn and Benny had long harboured desires to craft songs for stage musicals, and tested the waters here with "The Girl With The Golden Hair". The on-tour live version comprised four songs: the three here plus "Get On The Carousel". This last number was however deemed too instrumental-based and repetitive to make a suitable album cut (so parts of its melody were pilfered for "Hole In Your Soul".) The musical's story, as such, followed a young girl who dreamed of glory as a singer. Leaving her small-town roots for the big bad city, she finds fame and riches but soon learns they're not what she wanted and don't bring happiness. There are obvious, if glib, parallels to Agnetha's career arc here: we'll explore them in tandem with the relevant songs.

Agnetha was pregnant throughout 1977 with her and Bjorn's second child. Their son Christian was born in December. She began to prefer staying at home being a mum to flying around the world being a pop goddess. From this point on, she and Bjorn rowed like fury for eighteen months before bowing to the inevitable and splitting up. We'll come back to this cloud later.

> *" ABBA - THE ALBUM WAS TO PROVE THE THIRD BIGGEST SHIFTER OF '78, BEATEN ONLY BY THE PHENOMENA OF SATURDAY NIGHT FEVER AND GREASE. "*

Agnetha's pregnancy hadn't made the already fractious filming of *Abba – The Movie* any easier. Lasse Hallstrom had shot most of it as the group toured Australia in the spring of '77. It was Stig's idea: having witnessed the impact that Hallstrom's short-form videos had made, he was the one pushing for the movie as a far-reaching promotional tool. The band had records to make and were pretty exhausted, but once again submitted to Stig's Napoleonic – and, it has to be conceded, usually commercially vindicated – tendencies. *Abba – The Movie* was chiefly on-the-road footage, but Hallstrom was always trying to be imaginative, and it caught Australia's hysterical Abba-mania just at its peak. Agnetha only needed to wiggle her backside onstage and thousands of admirers turned to jelly. When the band played an open-air show to

25,000 in Sydney in a torrential thunderstorm, risking life, limb and electrocution (and loss of dignity when even Frida skidded over and went flying on her rear), they were applauded as gods.

Hallstrom, who also scripted, made a slick, well-produced 95-minute slice of visual entertainment from the footage acquired. He broke up the onstage scenes with fleeting glimpses of Benny, Bjorn, Agnetha and Frida backstage or signing autographs: there was no pretence at an exposé or a behind-the-scenes documentary. Or at the group doing any "acting". It aimed for the frothy appeal of The Beatles' *A Hard Day's Night*. Australian actors played cameo comic roles as shrieking fans or obsessed would-be interviewers.

Robert Hughes was cast as Ashley, a prat-falling radio D.J. pursuing the band across Australia in the hope of landing a scoop. Frida and Agnetha, the latter with pregnancy heavily disguised, were asked to flirt overtly with his character in a surreal dream sequence completely at odds with the rest of the movie. After all, as Agnetha pointed out, it was a "family" film: "You have to think about the young children watching." Hughes has since spoken of how he believed this would be his big break, making him an international star. It didn't. "Ashley" irritated the hell out of most viewers, and the picture did only moderately well. (In America, the movie didn't even open till 1979, although Hallstrom's own celebrity as a "serious" film-maker has since made it something to be regarded as an "ironic" museum piece.

So, this double-whammy concept of album and movie didn't quite match up to Stig's hopes, at least in commercial terms – the terms that meant the most to him. The album couldn't match the figures

of *Arrival*, but then few records could. When some critics described it as a "failure", Bjorn and Benny understandably got snippy and quoted statistics. It's safe to say that Agnetha and Frida were too shattered from the relentless schedule to worry too much about the odd thousand sales here or there: Agnetha, in particular, was beginning to focus more and more on other matters, closer to home.

For Bjorn and Benny, though, it was an important musical statement. If *The Album* didn't hang together as well as some of their other works, that was because they were still creatively ambitious. *Abba – The Album* varied in tone and texture, sometimes from track to track. Abba were stretching in all directions – from musical theatre to laid-back Californian "drive-time" adult-orientated rock. Stig's involvement in lyric-writing was now minimal, practically zero Bjorn was from now on the man in that department. Here, you can hear the results of a turbulent year, where the workaholism of Ulvaeus and Andersson still shone through, and still – at the very least – produced textbook singles. They were still chock-full of surprises.

Eagle

The first, and most obvious, indication that Abba had been soaking up some Californian soft rock, and at five minutes and fifty seconds something of a grand statement as an opening track. (Though this album had other – and conflicting – grand statements in store). With its big, lush, panoramic feel, "Eagle" is led by shimmering key-boards of a kind you might have heard in records by such practitioners of the form as Toto, Asia and REO Speedwagon. There's an easy, relaxed light-funk feel which veils the song's ambition of scope. The vocals are clearer than ever, evidently tidied up for American radio consumption. And this is no bad thing, as Frida and Agnetha sound absolutely great, and hungry for drama.

This is one of the few times (up to this point) where Abba let a groove, well... groove – they just allow it to coast, and don't fret too much about filling every second with magic tricks. The guitars are cool rather than constipated. Then in the final couple of minutes, the production really kicks in, and a level of plushness is attained that wouldn't shame Trevor Horn (the Eighties production guru behind such acts as Frankie Goes To Hollywood, ABC, Seal, etc).

Bjorn's lyrics were inspired by a reading of *Jonathan Livingston Seagull*, the bizarrely popular hippie novel of the period written by Richard Bach, a forerunner of "new age" philosophies. He took some flak for one or two of the platitudes therein. "Eagle" featured prominently in the movie, in a scene in which a special effects gadget borrowed fresh from the set of *Superman* was eagerly – if somewhat naively – used.

" *EAGLE* IS LED BY SHIMMERING KEYBOARDS OF A KIND YOU MIGHT HAVE HEARD IN RECORDS BY SUCH PRACTITIONERS OF THE FORM AS TOTO, ASIA AND REO SPEEDWAGON. "

Take a Chance On Me

From the initial "t-k-cha" (which came into Bjorn's head while out jogging), through the stunning set piece of the vocals-only interplay over the opening twenty seconds or so, this is a masterpiece. Quivering guitar beckons in the band, and though the music is basic, fairground stuff, that's all it needs to be. The melody surges

inexorably, and the breathtaking backing vocal arrangement builds and builds until it's almost unbearably involving. The pre-chorus tease is classic Abba, the call-and-response ("that's all I ask of you honey") is very nearly sexy, and the way the word "magic" is sung – so high! – is a thing of beauty. The ripples just keep getting bigger and bigger.

Benny took issue with some of Bjorn's lyrics, which he deemed lame – specifically "we could go

dancing, we could go walking". Bjorn put his foot down and explained that he was really getting rather good at knowing what worked with what in the pop arena. The pair were nothing if not democratic – Bjorn could also criticise Benny's music without the pair falling out – and peace prevailed.

In America, when you say Abba, they still respond by citing, if not "Dancing Queen", then "Take A Chance On Me". In the UK it stormed to number one in February '78, by means of a timely displacement of Brotherhood Of Man's latest Abba rip-off, "Figaro". It stayed at the top for a relatively brief three weeks, giving way to Kate Bush's debut single, "Wuthering Heights".

" IN THE UK IT STORMED TO NUMBER ONE IN FEBRUARY '78... IT STAYED AT THE TOP FOR A RELATIVELY BRIEF THREE WEEKS. "

One Man, One Woman

Punk? Disco? The year of 1977 had other things on its mind in some quarters. This is one of Abba's better big showboating ballads, with Frida in fine voice even if guided a little uncomfortably towards West End musical territory, with some hammy, over-precise diction. Luckily, Agnetha's more rasping tones help greatly when they come in. The guitars are again very Eagles-influenced, very of their time (in those quarters where punk and disco didn't register, anyway).

How much you can read into the lyrics *vis-à-vis* the band's now-rocky real life relationships is debatable, although many point to it as another early example of Bjorn confiding in the public. Despite the pessimistic opening, "No smiles, not a single word at the breakfast table… you leave and you slam the door", it resolves itself with some hope: "Somehow we'll help each other through the hard times…"

The Name Of The Game

The cool, shuffling bassline ushers in another shift of gear – both within the album and within Abba's hit singles legacy. The vocals are hushed, restrained but compelling – "I was an impossible case" – and the acoustic guitars emphasising the chorus emulate "Knowing Me, Knowing You". "I have no friends, no-one to see…" gives a hint of tears-of-a-clown loneliness-despite-fame which reappears (for Agnetha) in the "mini-musical"

section. For once the backing vocals are brilliantly subtle rather than brilliantly strident, and the horn crying over the fade is dextrously poignant. Plenty of space is left here – there's enough room, yet enough suggestion, for you to bring your own emotions to it. Many years after first hearing it, you can still pick up new facets of this fragile, flawless production. Here it's as if Abba now believe they're good, rather than just cunning; that they're artists, not just craftsmen.

> " …THE BACKING VOCALS ARE BRILLIANTLY SUBTLE RATHER THAN BRILLIANTLY STRIDENT, AND THE HORN CRYING OVER THE FADE IS DEXTROUSLY POIGNANT. "

In 1996 hip-hop megastars Fugees asked if they could sample the intro line for their song "Rumble In The Jungle", used as the theme song for the Mohammed Ali tribute movie *When We Were Kings*. Abba notoriously rarely allow any sampling of their songs whatsoever, but, perhaps thrilled to gain some hip-hop cred, said yes this one time.

Move On

The spoken male into and flute-ish pipes cause you to fear one of Abba's almighty lapses of taste as this begins, but when the girls come in beautifully to get a purchase on the melody, matters improve radically. Inventive percussion drives a sweet, sun-soaked number, whose only real *faux pas* is that irksome keyboard solo. And there's a classic example of Agnetha and Frida's characteristic sibilance on the word "treasure" – make that "treassssure". The "la la la" bit shouldn't work but does, and again the quartet's genius for multi-part vocal arrangements kisses glory. Later chosen as one of the songs re-recorded for the Spanish market, "Move On" marked one of the last times that Stig had any input into the lyrics. And probably his crucial contribution was, as on many occasions before, to suggest a catch-all title.

Peculiarly, "The Name Of The Game" was at first second favourite to "Hole In Your Soul" as the single to serve as a trailer to the album. In Australia that plan was switched just days before release. Then, when "The Name Of The Game" – too subtle? – stuttered down under, some record company types did a see-I-told-you-so schtick. Everywhere else, however, this slinky gem did just fine.

> "THE 'LA LA LA' BIT SHOULDN'T WORK BUT DOES, AND AGAIN THE QUARTET'S GENIUS FOR MULTI-PART VOCAL ARRANGEMENTS KISSES GLORY."

Hole In Your Soul

They're "rock'n'roll"-ing again! And this time they get away with it. While the West Coast influence is discernible in both lead and rhythm guitar styles, there's also a flicker of the British glam stomp sound that Abba had once adored (and still did). The opening riffery and drum patterns are straight out of Elton John's "Saturday Night's Alright For Fighting", and the girls' switches between ultra-high and only very high are the first time they've done Pinky & Perky in some years. There's a brief cameo for poor old frustrated (but I'm a singer too!) Bjorn. The words are Abba at their most embarrassing – evidently, some of their friends who aren't global superstars do ghastly menial working-class jobs like chauffeuring and office work, but it's okay, because they still like to, um, rock-'n'roll. Then the gals declare, "we sure play it cool". Anyone who declares that they "sure play it cool" is a long, long way off ever being cool, but still…

Then we arrive at the thoroughly unexpected middle eight, where everything cuts out and the girls just sing a capella, angelically. It's startling. It's another trailer telling us that Bjorn and Benny are coming over all "rock opera", like The Who in slippers, very soon. And the way the word "soul" goes suddenly up, up and away is madder than a spider in pyjamas.

Soon something of a barnstorming live favourite, this was a partial rewrite of excerpts from "The Girl With The Golden Hair".

The Girl With The Golden Hair: 3 Scenes From a Mini-Musical

Bjorn and Benny keenly hoped their ambitious mini-musical, the show-stopping finale of the Abba live shows at this time, would stop them being pigeonholed as brainless popsters. On the other hand, they were dimly aware that it could backfire, and they'd be pigeonholed as anodyne AOR. In the planning stages, *Abba – The Movie* was going to centre around its "story", but time was limited. Tim Rice and Andrew Lloyd Webber were in the ascendant, big-time, with *Jesus Christ Superstar* and *Evita* proving colossal money-spinners. It reveals the curious machinations of the Swedish notion of "hip" that Bjorn and Benny envied Rice and Lloyd Webber. The biggest pop group in the world, they thought *Evita* was "cool". Let's not be too sneering though: it was perceived as cooler then than it is now. Bear with me while I pick myself up from bending over backwards.

So 1977's stage "vision" of "The Girl With The Golden Hair", as performed in Abba's concerts, was limited. Agnetha and Frida donned identical blonde wigs – bright enough to be spotted from Row Z – and impersonated (as best they could) clockwork dolls. They were supposed to be representing contrasting personalities within the same woman. A pompous "actorly" thesp hired from the Royal Shakespeare Company, Francis Matthews, announced links in the "plot". He admitted frankly to "mixed feelings" concerning the work's merits. He later became director of the Greenwich Theatre in London.

This "plot" – young starry-eyed girl has her innocent dreams corrupted by fame and greed – was about as incongruous and inappropriate as you could imagine for an up-for-it Abba audience who were there to clap along to the jolly hits and ogle Agnetha's rear. As a climax to the gigs it was, as they say, a real downer. As art, it was less than dazzlingly original, and half-cocked.

> " *ABBA – THE MOVIE* WAS GOING TO CENTRE AROUND ITS 'STORY', BUT TIME WAS LIMITED. "

Agnetha's "Thank You For The Music", despite the song's overt pleasantness, awkwardly echoed her own teenage dreams of becoming a pop sweetheart through pure talent and a coy smile. When Frida sang "I Wonder" (po-facedly subtitled "Departure" with a nod to *Arrival*), there were haunting resonances of her own background, as she'd left her husband and children to pursue musical fame. And "I'm A Marionette" saw both women jerking like puppets on strings (damn those Eurovision motifs!) while complaining about being bossed around and turned into commodities for heartless moneymen and voracious consumers. Challenging stuff, given the context, from the not-so-shallow Swedes.

Audiences, not knowing what in the name of sweet Jesus was going on, tolerated it. Critics loathed it. Even Abba later allowed that the concept was rushed and possibly botched. At one show, Frida's wig fell off. She quickly pushed it back on… back to front. Abba were clean living by rock star standards, but have never denied that they liked a drink or five. They've since confessed that they drank like fish after some of these particular shows.

Bjorn reworked many of the lyrics before they were recorded for the album.

sing". And then counter accusations of bragging with: "I'm so grateful and proud". "Thank You For The Music" is one of the cheesiest songs ever written, but if you're going to be cheesy, you may as well be the unapologetic epitome of cheese…

> "THIS WAS VERY LLOYD WEBBER, VERY WEST END, VERY BROADWAY IF YOU LIKE THAT KIND OF THING."

1. Thank You For The Music

Very over-familiar now, and one of those "big" anthems which prospective pop idols have to murder as a televised rite of passage. This was very Lloyd Webber, very West End, very Broadway if you like that kind of thing. Agnetha tells her story. Massed choirs join in, less than realistically. You have to wonder how much input she had in Bjorn's lyrics as she sings, "I am the girl with the golden hair". Presumably she was okay with singing, "I'm nothing special, in fact I'm a bit of a bore/If I tell a joke, you've probably heard it before". And if she was, that'd be because then she gets to brag about her "talent, a wonderful thing/ Everyone listens when I start to

2. I Wonder (departure)

Frida's turn. Our golden-haired girl leaves her hometown in search of fame, and wonders if she's doing the right thing. Very camp and stage-y, this, with Bjorn and Benny marking out a test run for their later-life careers. The power-ballad chorus does its job, and the luvvie pronunciation of, "Who the hell am I?" could win awards if aped by Elaine Paige or Barbara Dickson. As would the big, arms-akimbo, head-tossed-back final sob of "It can't go wrong!" Benny's piano-playing is like Liberace possessing Richard Clayderman. When you think back to the album's AOR beginnings, what a very schizophrenic record this is.

3. I'm a Marionette

To reiterate: did Agnetha approve these lyrics? Now she's a puppet, a doll, who hates fame. Was Björn making mileage from her diaries? Does that make him a caring, concerned husband, trying to understand her angst? Or a completely callous swine? In fairness, he was probably straining to be the former...

The burbling, suspenseful intro – at least it's not another power-ballad, you think – leads into a strangely aggressive number, its semi-tragic lyrics of disillucionment poured across a pseudo-classical, prog-rock howl. "It's insane!" it yells. You're inclined to agree. Benny's trying too hard to prove Abba aren't just a singles band, but this is hard to like, however intricate and unpredictable. You could play it to Abba laymen and they'd never guess what band it was in a million years. After the big (big) finish, you mutter to yourself: *that* was a touch deranged.

> **"IT SCORES TEN FOR AMBITION AND DARING, LESS THAN TEN FOR COHESION OR SPARKLE."**

Overall, "Three Scenes From A Mini-Musical" is a soundtrack to a non-existent movie, and as intriguing and frustrating as that suggests. It scores ten for ambition and daring, less than ten for cohesion or sparkle. Yes, we know Sweden produced Ingmar Bergman, and other dark, broody, morose types. Yet whatever Abba might have said, no matter how many times they banged their wannabe-serious-musos' heads against the wall, what they were best at was creating fantastic pop music. When they did that – "Take A Chance On Me" and "The Name Of The Game" were just two more examples – they were simply world-beaters.

Still, nobody could now accuse them of resting on their laurels. Within two months of completing *The Album*, they began work on the next. Another shift of direction was required before this one came together. Abba, having almost unwittingly hit dancefloor pay dirt with "Dancing Queen", were about to go out-and-out disco.

BONUS TRACKS on 2001 reissue:
Thank You For The Music (Doris Day Version)

The original recorded version of the song luxuriates in a Twenties, ragtime feel, one which has you whistling "As Time Goes By" and "Smoke Gets In Your Eyes". It lopes along – languid, likeable – and its breezy understatement's refreshing set against the bloated, better-known rendition. Agnetha listened to a bunch of Doris Day records to find the right "voice". She does well, but the put-on accent slips fleetingly like that of an imperfect actor. The group preferred the now-famous version, so this gathered dust in a vault for nearly two decades before being first unearthed for the 1994 box set that bore its name.

VOULEZ-VOUS 1979

Recorded March 1978 - March 1979, at Polar, Metronome, Glen and Marcus studios, Stockholm, and Criteria, Miami USA.

Produced by Benny Andersson and Bjorn Ulvaeus. Engineered by Michael Tretow.

Musicians: Benny Andersson (keyboards, synths); Bjorn Ulvaeus (guitars, banjos); Janne Schaffer (guitars); Rutger Gunnarsson (bass, string arrangements); Arnold Paserio (bass); Mike Watson (bass); Ola Brunkert (drums); Rolf Alex (drums); Joe Galdo (drums); Malando Gassama (percussion); Ake Sundquist (percussion); Paul Harris (piano); Ish Ledesma (guitars); George Terry (guitars); Lasse Wellander (guitars); Halldor Palsson (sax); Johan Stengard (sax); Lars O. Carlsson (sax); Kajtek Wojciechowski (sax); Nils Landgren (sax); Christer Danielsson (bass trombone); Jan Risberg (oboe); Anders Eljas (string and horn arrangements); International School Of Stockholm Choir.

Vocals by Abba.

AS GOOD AS NEW

VOULEZ-VOUS

I HAVE A DREAM

ANGEL EYES

THE KING HAS LOST HIS CROWN

DOES YOUR MOTHER KNOW

IF IT WASN'T FOR THE NIGHTS

CHIQUITITA

LOVERS (LIVE A LITTLE LONGER)

KISSES OF FIRE

Bonus tracks on 2001 Reissue:

SUMMER NIGHT CITY

LOVELIGHT

GIMME! GIMME! GIMME! (A MAN AFTER MIDNIGHT)

ABBA – THE ALBUM DIDN'T QUITE HAVE AS MANY FANS AND CRITICS BREAKING OUT IN RASHES OF SUPERLATIVES AS BJORN AND BENNY MIGHT HAVE WISHED. THEY REACTED IN TYPICAL (FOR THEM) STYLE, THROWING THEMSELVES BACK INTO SOMETHING APPROACHING A WORKAHOLIC ROUTINE, AND WERE WRITING AGAIN JUST A MONTH OR SO LATER.

Despite this, Abba's sixth album didn't enjoy an easy birth, released six months later than originally envisaged, but when it did eventually emerge, they had successfully tapped into the prevalent disco grooves of the era and come up with another sweet shift in direction. *Voulez-Vous*, hugely influenced by the Bee Gees' *Saturday Night Fever* masterpieces, is sometimes dismissed as one of the group's lesser works, but there are many of us who find its sleek, sexy, calculated sheen irresistible. It is as close as Abba ever came to their sex album.

Then again, this being Abba, the record displayed a cute form of sonic schizophrenia. Iconic pop slush-sters "I Have A Dream" and "Chiquitita" aren't exactly full of funk, and "Does Your Mother Know?" might be rollicking good fun, but it is also as daft as a very daft brush.

The gestation period for the album was also a trying time for Bjorn and Agnetha, and, inversely, a celebratory one for Benny and Frida. The latter couple, after being engaged for nine years, finally married in October 1978. The ceremony, at their local church, was an almost perversely private affair – even Bjorn and Agnetha weren't invited. Perhaps Benny and Frida were simply being diplomatic: by January '79, Abba's more petite half had announced their divorce, which had been on the cards for a while. They were, however, perfectly content to carry on working together, and we'll look into how they managed this shortly. Bjorn's lyrics on the *Voulez-Vous* album are markedly less innocent and pristine, and enjoyably more sweaty and lusty.

As songwriters, Benny and Bjorn weren't finding Sweden inspirational. They'd introduced American stylings on *Abba – The Album*, and they found the dearth of decent music on Swedish radio frustrating. So they took a trip to the Bahamas, which proved crucial to *Voulez-Vou*s. Motivated by what they heard on their working holiday, they returned full of fire, and at least half the subsequent tracks were recorded in a burst towards the end of the sessions.

They also took another trip, to Miami, following in the Bee Gees' footsteps, and hooked up with a hot disco band, Foxy, for the thumping title track, assisted by legendary producer Tom Dowd. Dowd had already worked wonders with everyone from Dusty Springfield and Aretha Franklin to Rod Stewart. The album grooved to the top of the charts in over ten countries as Abba's music joined in with the disco inferno of early 1979. It occupied the British top spot from mid-May onwards, spending a total of 43 weeks on the chart (coincidentally, exactly the same number of weeks as *Super Trouper* did eighteen months later). The cover shot was intended to present Bjorn, Benny, Agnetha and Frida as "sophisticated" night-clubbers – but in fact they looked decidedly tacky, and more like a quartet of suburbanites warming up for an exciting evening of key swapping.

By November '79, Abba's *Greatest Hits Volume Two* was holding off all-comers in those album charts. The record-buying punters loved Abba's hit-packed compilations, and they were as potent a commercial force as ever. Yet Stateside, *Voulez-Vous* peaked at number nineteen.

If, musically, Abba were slipping into a slinkier gear, their personal lives were pulling in the kind of publicity that they would have preferred to do without. Bjorn and Agnetha's sad announcement of their impending separation was no surprise to close observers Benny and Frida, but even Stig – from whom the four had drifted apart a little – was stunned when told. Neither did they enjoy breaking the news to five-and-a-half-year-old Linda.

The media, of course, went crazy when Bjorn and Agnetha dropped the bombshell. The couple stressed that their decision was as amicable as could be under the circumstances, that the custody of the children would be shared, and that they hadn't rushed into it, but Agnetha in particular hated the frenzy of flashbulbs that then followed her everywhere. The media's myth of the two cuddly happy couples was blown, and that media wasn't at first too pleased. But when Bjorn found himself a new flame within a matter of weeks, and a little later Agnetha did too, the media merrily moved on, embracing these fresh new angles as the media is wont to do.

> "THE ALBUM GROOVED TO THE TOP OF THE CHARTS IN OVER TEN COUNTRIES AS ABBA'S MUSIC JOINED IN WITH THE DISCO INFERNO OF EARLY 1979."

This didn't prevent a storm of rumours and gossip. The world's press didn't need much encouraging to steam in with the "Abba Split" headlines. Perhaps this steeled the resolve of the group to keep going and prove them wrong. After years of growing up in public together, and two kids, Bjorn and Agnetha were at the very least good friends, and still shared an abiding passion for their music.

For Abba fans – if it's not too callous a point to make – the split reaped a happier harvest. Benny and Frida (and indeed Bjorn and Agnetha) have since remarked that the atmosphere within the group became a lot better, rather than worse, once Bjorn and Agnetha called it a day on the personal level. A lot of fit-to-burst tension was dissipated, and the pair seem to have been able to function just fine as a working team afterwards. Bjorn's gone so far as to say it meant he could now advise and direct Agnetha in recordings without her taking his every opinion as an attack. The musicians who played onstage with Abba have sworn that, even at close proximity, you wouldn't have noticed that anything had changed within their rapport once the live set kicked in: another night, another city.

It also meant that Bjorn's lyrics were considerably looser and more louche. *Voulez-Vous* is an album with a definitively "disco" heart – it's all about flirting, pick-ups, one night stands and physical attraction. It's casually sexy, or sometimes confessionally gauche. Either way, it's much much more intriguing than those songs about sitting in palm trees and banging a boomerang, or whatever. Agnetha too seems to sing with more clarity, confidence and purpose. As for the newly-weds, Benny and Frida, they too are clearly having a very good time.

Enough brow furrowing about relationships. Let's get down and dirty (okay, it's still Abba, but everything's relative) with the funk. Despite the saccharin sentimentality of the big blubbing ballads, *Voulez-Vous* is primarily an athletic, amorous album that only just restrains itself, through an in-built sense of proper decorum, from panting heavily and adding "…coucher avec moi?"

As Good As New

One of the greatest beginnings of any Abba album. Benny executes one of his keyboard flourishes, then – thwack! – we're into a brisk disco rhythm, all notions of West Coast hippie-dom cast aside. This is one of the songs that Benny and Bjorn wrote in a prolific period after returning from Miami. Instantly, we can hear that Abba have learned fast and got it right – there is no lame bandwagon-jumping here. The bass is furiously funky and the clipped, precise tempo shows a fine understanding of what made the men behind Chic and Sister Sledge (Nile Rodgers and Bernard Edwards) so influential. There are inevitably a few trademark Abba chord sequences, but generally these aren't allowed to over-complicate the groove – not on this terrific track, anyway. The same goes for the strings, which are kept subjugated to the surge – in fact, everything kow-tows to the bass, which is how it should be in this genre.

Agnetha's vocals are pure disco, too – passionate, yearning, but stopping short of any real rawness or roughness. The "ma-ma-ma-ma" hook is the killer. The theme – in short; I thought we were through, baby, but we're not – perhaps reveals that Bjorn and Agnetha were experiencing ups and downs and false dawns until very late in the day…

In subsequent live shows, Bjorn's misjudged onstage quips that the title referred directly to Agnetha were regarded as unsubtle and tactless, especially in middle America. One reviewer said simply: "Ugh".

Voulez-Vous

Five minutes of utterly unabashed sex-drenched magic. After a surreal, almost Arabic or Indian winding motif that wouldn't be out of place on a record by Monsoon or even Siouxsie & The Banshees, "Voulez-Vous" clicks seamlessly into twinkling uber-disco, led by a slightly shifty rhythm guitar, a strutting bass, and stabbing horns which pre-empt the Eighties' "new" white-boy funk. The faultless build-up and drama of the galaxy-grabbing melody shows how cleverly Abba have adjoined their own strengths to the genre – after unwittingly stumbling on the glorious "Dancing Queen" (Icelandic star Björk's favourite record of all time), Abba are living the groove for real. "Voulez-Vous" – very much a product of its time – now sounds classically, rather than sadly, dated. It even has one of those "twelve-inch" "breakdown" sections that were then so in vogue. "Masters of the scene", indeed.

There are chords as big and spacious as the planets, and the latest in a proud line of impish "a-ha!" hooks. The surge into the chorus confirms this as one of the great soulless one-night-stand disco anthems. It's truly impossible to keep still to. Abba, let us not forget, have a humungous gay following, stretching way beyond the members of Erasure. The song's Hallstrom video emphasised the "clubbing" feel.

We must thank Foxy for much of this. At Criteria Studios, Miami, Bjorn, Benny and Michael Tretow (whose input and loyalty had recently been rewarded by an undemanded but very generous financial agreement with the band) worked with several of the studio's hot engineers. Together they assembled a backing band drawn from members of Foxy, who'd just had an American top ten hit with the disco gem, "Get Off". You can hear the success of the result. (The same line-up attempted "If It Wasn't For The Nights", although not so convincingly). Abba then finished the track off back in Stockholm.

> ## " VOULEZ-VOUS DIDN'T SMASH THE AMERICAN MARKET AS WIDE OPEN AS THE BAND HAD HOPED. THE SINGLE STALLED AT NUMBER 80. "

"Voulez-Vous" didn't smash the American market as wide open as the band had hoped. The single stalled at number 80. Even when flipped over as a damage limitation exercise, "Angel Eyes" only lifted it to 64. America, even now, was the land that refused to buckle to Abba, yet in the era of Bee Gees blockbusters and Blondie's "Heart Of Glass"

(not to mention The Village People's "YMCA"), the US's frostiness was surprising. Britain propelled "Voulez-Vous/Angel Eyes" into the top three... but not to number one.

"This girl means business so I'll offer her a drink... take it now or leave it, now is all we get... nothing promised, no regrets... you know what I mean..." Hang on a minute! Could it be that raunchy pick-up merchants Abba were just too saucy for wholesome family consumption?

I Have A Dream

Oh. Scratch that theory. Abba were nothing if not calculating. Gross slush-fests like this irredeemably (and tragically, to some of our ears) broke up the flow and feel of a hugely promising album, but they certainly did their job in keeping the middle-of-the-road granny-and-grandkids audience onside. When released as a single at the end of the year, it reassured and comforted any wavering old school Abba fans, who sat back comfortably in anticipation of an anodyne Eighties.

"I Have A Dream" harked back to the boys' unfortunate schlager roots. It was the first time any voices other than Abba's had featured on an Abba record, in the shape of a Stockholm children's choir. To British listeners of a certain age, this lends it a terribly distressing resemblance to the one-off Christmas hit, "Grandma" by St.Winifred's Girls School Choir. Indeed, "I Have A Dream" was targeted at the festive market. When writing it, Benny would urge friends to sing along – he took their compliance as an indication that it was a winner. Today, it only makes us think of dreary Pop Idol runners-up, Demis Roussos, and "Fernando" without the style and emotion. Martin Luther King it ain't.

Number one in Belgium, Switzerland and Holland; number two in Britain. Linda, Bjorn and Agnetha's daughter, joined the choir onstage at a Vegas gig. You win some, you…

Angel Eyes

If "Angel Eyes" being lumped together as a double A-side with "Voulez-Vous" seems an odd pairing, given the strength of both tracks, the struggle to impact on America perhaps explains it. Or maybe Abba feared that disco-sceptics wouldn't take to "Voulez-Vous", but might like this more "Abba-esque" ditty. In the UK both songs were popular, even if the almost simultaneous release of a Roxy Music single named "Angel Eyes" – also a shiny experiment in modern dance – confused one or two of us. (It's not an uncommon title, as Jennifer Lopez and Wet Wet Wet will also vouch).

> "ABBA FEARED THAT DISCO-SCEPTICS WOULDN'T TAKE TO *VOULEZ-VOUS*, BUT MIGHT LIKE THIS MORE 'ABBA-ESQUE' DITTY."

These days, "Angel Eyes" actually sounds more Motown than disco, its driving beat swept along by a deliciously intricate melody line. It's yet another Abba nugget that, once heard, won't leave your head for days. After another "a-ha-ha" refrain, it stutters to get going but is warmed up by the pop drama of Benny's chord pattern. There can be no doubt that Stock, Aitken and Waterman are familiar with this tune.

And what's with the lyrics? The story of a lover-man who is irresistible but not so innocent seems to be a case of Bjorn boosting his self-image, loudly. Divorce will do funny things to a man.

The King Has Lost His Crown

Frida's glory shot sounds very much like the kind of thing Barbra Streisand was soon to do on her massively successful collaboration with Bee Gees' Barry Gibb, "Guilty". It's sultry but not *too* sultry, rhythmic but laid-back. And the intro section is nothing if not reminiscent of Cliff Richard's late Seventies' hits. Scarily, so is Frida's breathy vocal… let's be kind and compare the texture to the tropical temptations of Olivia Newton-John's "Physical"…

There's still a hint of schlager in the tune, but the movie theme guitars pick it up. British pop-soul maestros Hot Chocolate did this sort of thing so much better, though. They'd never have suffered the "disaster and disgrace!" lapse, which is pure Lloyd Webber. But Frida's self-confidence increases as the song moves along, and the production's tasty enough to keep it fluid. The big

high note towards the end is the most obvious Bee Gees tribute in an album packed with obvious Bee Gees "tributes"...

Does Your Mother Know

Bjorn sings lead vocals, everybody! Calm your-selves! And, with a potential embarrassment level bordering on the excruciating (which is up there, even for dear old Bjorn) he sings about fancying an underage hottie. And they go and release this thing as a single, in spring 1979. And it only goes and becomes a respectably-sized hit in about a zillion countries…

One of the last songs written for the album, "Does Your Mother Know" has been described by acclaimed Abba biographer Carl Magnus Palm as "a daring tribute to cross-generational flirting in big city nightclubs". Well, either that or Bjorn's inner, long-repressed heavy metal head-banger got the better of him after an ill-advised tipple or two. What on earth would Agnetha have thought? Following in the tradition of Vladimir Nabokov's *Lolita* (though marginally less literary) and Gary Puckett & The Union Gap's Sixties smash "Young Girl" (though marginally less epic), Bjorn's hot-under-the-collar homage to naughty schoolgirls is a confounding curio. "You're so hot, teasing me…" Of course he advocates restraint and abstinence, but not before weighing up the options rather salaciously. "I can

dance with you honey/ If you think it's funny/I can chat with you baby/ Flirt a little, maybe…" Oh dear - steady on there, Uncle Bjorn, or we shan't be inviting you to any more family christenings…

"Take it easy", he decides. "That's no way to go." Phew. Just as well, really: the old-fashioned values image of Abba had taken enough knocks in recent months. The "take it easy" section was actually borrowed from an old composition – "Dream World" – which Benny and Bjorn had had lying around for ages, and slipped into this thumping pop-rocker which, ironically, got people onto the dancefloor as eagerly as any of the disco tracks. "Does Your Mother Know" has since acquired a degree of so-naff-it's-cool ironic élan. People say that of a lot of Abba's hits, but in fact most of them are cool because they're cool, are loved because they're great. This one, though, really is where irony wins out. Bjorn never sang lead vocals on a single again.

> **"DOES YOUR MOTHER KNOW HAS SINCE ACQUIRED A DEGREE OF SO-NAFF-IT'S-COOL IRONIC ÉLAN… PEOPLE SAY THAT OF A LOT OF ABBA'S HITS."**

And yet… years later, ultra-credible rock giants R.E.M, chose to cover "Does Your Mother Know?" Doubtless they were inspired by its stonking back-beat, its glammy guitar riff, the girls guzzling the helium again for the backing vocals, and its all-round celebration of the newly single man's physical urges.

Abba's version peaked at number four in anal, buttoned-up Britain.

If It Wasn't For The Nights

Getting us back on track, this gorgeous slice of disco shuffle cuts to the album's motivational core again. It has a lovely feel – bringing to mind lofty names as diverse as Barry White, Love Unlimited Orchestra, Chic of course, even Curtis Mayfield – and the deft guitar glide is touch-perfect. As George McRae's "Rock Your Baby" had inspired "Dancing Queen", perhaps his less well-known but equally airy "It's Been So Long" influenced this underrated classic. And, again, there's no denying the echo of the Bee Gees' productions - possibly Yvonne Elliman's "Love Me" or "If I Can't Have You"…

It's one of Bjorn's best lyrics too, more grown-up than usual in a sort of I'm-partying-hard-because-I-need-to-forget-my-heart's-breaking way. The girls' vocals are superb, and, for once, not tweaked up too shrilly. "I've got my business to get me through the day", it confides, "… I'd be doing all right if it wasn't for the nights." The multiple voices on the call-and-response of "Its bad – oh so bad" are a stroke of genius. It's tempting to say you

might not recognise this track as Abba, so authentic is its veneer of disco cool, but then the "aaaah" backing vocals come in, and you know it can only be one band in the world. This is a delicious dance-floor reverie, nonetheless.

Mooted as an early single, it lost out to the safer bet "Chiquitita". Shame. Benny and Bjorn weren't convinced the groove handled all the complicated chord changes too smoothly. When subsequent live shows began with "Voulez-Vous" then kicked straight into this, thrilling audiences, they may have had second thoughts. One of those rare and wonderful blessed pop songs that make heart-break sound joyous, and the best ever non-single Abba album track by some miles.

Chiquitita

Without wishing to drone on about maudlin ballads for grannies that kill the mood again, here's a maudlin ballad for grannies that kills the mood. Inevitably, once again, it was a huge commercial success. In the UK it peaked at number two in February '79, only kept off the top spot by "Heart Of Glass" by Blondie. Originally "Chiquitita" was called "In The Arms Of Rosalita", and featured less Agnetha and more Frida but, as so often, the perfectionists Bjorn and Benny refashioned it before letting it loose into public scrutiny.

The United Nations had nominated '79 as the "Year Of The Child", and organised a gala show – A Gift Of Song – to be performed (and filmed for broadcast) in the UN Assembly Hall, in New York, in January. Abba were asked to take part, and donated the royalties from "Chiquitita" to UNICEF. They played the show alongside such diverse names as The Bee Gees, Olivia Newton John, Donna Summer, Earth, Wind & Fire, Rod Stewart and John Denver, literally just a few days before Bjorn and Agnetha's divorce announcement. All the acts joined in for a rendition of Abba's "He Is Your Brother" – surprising even Abba, who were aware it wasn't their best-known composition.

The American record company took some stick for not immediately releasing "Chiquitita" as a single in order to capitalise on this showcase. They didn't get their act together until October, by which time the song could only scrape into the top thirty there, but it made number one in nine or ten other countries. A Spanish-language version sold half a million copies in Argentina, and was one of the biggest hits across South America in around a quarter of a century.

"AT BEST IT'S A WEAK SIMON AND GARFUNKEL, AT WORST IT'S SCHLAGER HIPPIES AT THE CIRCUS."

"Chiquitita" – which sounds uncomfortably like something you'd find halfway down a Tex-Mex menu – is a clomping, big lighters-in-the-air ballad: y'know, a "song of hope". At best it's a weak Simon and Garfunkel, at worst it's schlager hippies at the circus. It's as far from disco, or even rock, as it gets.

Songs like this may have got the cash registers pinging but they were also responsible for Abba's perceived uncoolness, certainly in England. If you were a teenager in Britain in the Seventies you sneered at such a song for its conformity, its refusal to rebel. Against *what*, you probably hadn't a clue, but you knew it bored you, and it wasn't sexy.

If, however, you lived in South America or any Spanish-speaking nation, this was your favourite song ever.

Lovers (Live A Little Longer)

This was one of the few cuts that Abba got down early in the *Voulez-Vous* sessions (along with "Lovelight"), before hitting writers' block. Frida sings this funk-lite charmer, quite seductively for her. Lyrically, it's a helpful medical broadcast from the newly frisky (and soon spoken-for-again) Bjorn. Benny's keyboards swoosh grandly across hungry, stealthy, stalking rhythms and that Bee Gees influence is happily discernible again. As ever, there are dazzling hook lines, and there's a quite magnificent extended "hmmmmmmm" from a freed-up Frida before her entrance to the second verse. "Makin' love is a dynamite drug", she exhorts, "so why don't we start right away?" So, Abba as a seminal influence on the careers of Prince and Madonna, anyone?

Kisses Of Fire

More lust and passion, which here are "burning, burning" and rather marvellously rhymed with "I'm on the point of no returning". The soft voices usher us in, then bam! – we're into another honed disco groove thang. The keyboards shimmer with a nod to Giorgio Moroder's then-radical Donna Summer creations (such as "I Feel Love"). You can still hear the Eurovision habits in the vocal interplay, but now those Abba trade-marks are wrapped in sensuous velvet. Written during that crucial spell in the Bahamas, "Kisses Of Fire" was an unlikely b-side to "Does Your Mother Know" in some territories.

BONUS TRACKS on 2001 reissue:
Summer Night City

Considered a flop, by Abba's high standards, in the UK, "Summer Night City" peaked at number five in October 1978. Ironically, the chart-topping single at the time was the similarly-titled "Summer Nights", the John Travolta and Olivia Newton-John showpiece from *Grease*. While still the best-selling albums band, Abba lost their British singles act title to Boney M that year, and couldn't even finish above the likes of Darts, Boomtown Rats, ELO, Showaddywaddy and, er, The Smurfs. The ignominy of this single's "failure" meant that Abba originally left it off the album in a huff. Take that, you bad single! It should be noted that it was their biggest hit in Sweden since "Dancing Queen", and their first number one in Japan.

In retrospect, it's really not bad at all. It's rather groovy, in fact, having survived a troubled recording at Polar, but was perhaps too much of a departure too soon for the regular Abba audience. It's hot sweaty, suspenseful, and rumblingly bass-heavy. The vocals are a tad mashed and muddy, but the guitar hooks are crisp and it definitely captures that "feeling in the air" that it's after, of everyone being on the prowl and on the pull in the city's balmy night streets and bars. Bjorn, you are a hero.

And if that key change isn't one of the most obvious yet orgasmic in pop history, then Abba couldn't do pop. "That giant dynamo", indeed.

Lovelight

Recorded early, but left off the album at first, "Lovelight" emerged as the (far superior) b-side to "Chiquitita". Diehard Abba fans swear by it as one of the group's most underrated cuts of all. A mishmash of Euro-rock, vague disco and Mike Oldfield-ish guitar frills, it's just great. The chorus sounds like a million other things, but somehow like nothing but itself. Define that, and you define a top pop record. The "I don't want to lose you" refrain can only be defined as brilliance. In a perfect world, we'd dump the big ballads from *Voulez-Vous* and stick these big'n'beaty "bonus" tracks in their place. It would improve the cohesion and give the album a constant crackle.

Gimme! Gimme! Gimme! (A Man After Midnight)

As the years have passed, this – deemed an also-ran at the time – has come to be regarded as one of the all-time Abba camp classics. They even named a crap British TV sitcom after it. You know you're iconic when *that* happens.

The song was written after the album's release, as Abba rehearsed for their American and European tours of late 1979. A new single was required. This is what they came up with – just like that – and, released in October, it became a huge hit. It's arguably their disco pinnacle, what with the licentious, sexual frustration theme (which Agnetha sang with great relish), the guttural slap bass, the

twelve-inch stylings, the Moroder-influenced pulsebeat and the gratuitous flights of rock guitar. (Obscure rock sleaze-gurus The Leather Nun concocted a convincing cover in the late Eighties). With its delirious opening of "half past twelve", and liberal use of words like "depressed" and "gloom", it's a case of Bjorn finding the perfect lyrical concept to subvert the medium… a little, not too much. And let's give him credit for knowing what would bring the best out of Agnetha.

Yep, *Voulez-Vous* was Abba's sex album, all right, during their sex year. Agnetha (of the much-observed backside) and Frida had sported onstage "sexy" costumes for years, but remained a bit, well, pantomime, especially compared to Blondie's Debbie Harry's fusion of guts and glamour, which was reshaping the pop landscape and drawing up a new "women in rock" map. Now, though, with Madonna a mere wannabe and Kylie a babe in arms, Abba genuinely sounded firm but foxy. The album (mostly) works and Abba's disco period had worked like a dream. Consequently, as 1980 opened, Bjorn and Benny returned to Barbados to write new songs, believing that their Bahamas experiment might work out again…

"YEP, *VOULEZ-VOUS* WAS ABBA'S *SEX* ALBUM ALL RIGHT, DURING THEIR SEX YEAR."

SUPER TROUPER 1980

Recorded at Polar, Stockholm
(except "The Way Old Friends Do",
recorded live at Wembley Arena, London).

Produced by Benny Andersson and
Bjorn Ulvaeus, engineered by Michael Tretow.

Musicians: Benny Andersson
(keyboards, synthesisers); Bjorn Ulvaeus
(guitars); Rutger Gunnarsson (bass, string
arrangements); Mike Watson (bass);
Ola Brunkert (drums); Per Lindvall (drums);
Janne Schaffer (guitars); Lasse Wellander
(guitars); Lars O. Carlsson,
Kajtek Wojciechowski (saxophones);
Janne Kling (saxophones, flutes);
Ake Sundqvist (percussion).

Vocals by Abba.

SUPER TROUPER

THE WINNER TAKES IT ALL

ON AND ON AND ON

ANDANTE. ANDANTE

ME AND I

HAPPY NEW YEAR

OUR LAST SUMMER

THE PIPER

LAY ALL YOUR LOVE ON ME

THE WAY OLD FRIENDS DO

Bonus tracks on 2001 Reissue:

ELAINE

PUT ON YOUR WHITE SOMBRERO

THE EIGHTIES. A NEW DECADE, THEN. ABBA HAD RULED THE SEVENTIES COMMERCIALLY, OUTLIVING PROG ROCK, GLAM ROCK AND PUNK ROCK, THEN FORMING AN ALLIANCE OF CONVENIENCE WITH DISCO. BJORN, AGNETHA, BENNY AND FRIDA WERE GROWN-UPS NOW, HAVING DISCOVERED SEX AND DIVORCE, AND WANTED THE WORLD TO REALISE IT.

They were so very grown-up that they ditched the sex. And the disco. They wrote crafted pop again, with increasingly sincere lyrics from Bjorn. They dressed in a less satin'n'tat fashion, accepting – several years after everyone else – that the Seventies' glam wave was over. They still dressed... oddly, and started dressing older than their years. But they were no longer trying too hard.

It has been suggested that Bjorn and Benny were growing a little tired of perfect pop and it was coming too easily to them now. They'd cracked it, mastered

it, and now craved fresh challenges. These would come. The album after *Super Trouper* was to be their swansong, and was to be well weird. Which makes it all the more happy and poignant (simultaneously) that the enormously popular *Super Trouper* is "just" a fine pop album. It's as if Abba had decided to break open the quick-fix genius one last time, to seal their legacy with an icing-on-the-cake opus, before relaxing and letting go of the Abba moneymaking machine. Then they could go on to *really* take chances, risk upsetting some followers, and be themselves.

For Abba were no longer the chirpy simple Swedes of the *Waterloo* years. They were, by their own admission, jaded, and exhausted from keeping up appearances. Personally, emotionally and creatively tired. *Super Trouper* is an album (and a song) which explores an unorthodox theme – that of a band who are bored of fame. Within its first few lines, it's saying, "I was sick and tired of everything... All I do is eat and sleep and sing/Wishing every show was the last..." Officially, Abba were no longer having the time of their lives.

"I WAS SICK AND TIRED OF EVERYTHING... ALL I DO IS EAT AND SLEEP AND SING WISHING EVERY SHOW WAS THE LAST..."

Benny and Frida were still presenting an image of wedded bliss to the outside world but since they'd married they had, ironically, grown apart. As fiancées, they'd enjoyed a passionate relationship with lots of rows and romance, but now the passion was fading. Frida has since confessed that they would go out every night so as not to be stuck alone with each other. Agnetha, too, was struggling. Her two relationships in the eighteen months following her divorce from Bjorn had both ended. Her consistent role as the singer of Abba's "heartbreak" songs fuelled tabloid gossip, and she felt persecuted by the media. Her efforts to placate them only made matters worse, and she grew increasingly paranoid. (Except that, often, they really were out to get her).

Bjorn, at least, had found another chapter of happiness, marrying Lena Kallersjo in early January 1981. But by February, Benny and Frida were regretfully announcing divorce plans. For them, it was if their love had lived and died with Abba's inner spark. By March, Benny was living with another woman.

With all this going on at home, it's a wonder Abba found any time to go to the studio at all. But there was always this curious symbiosis between their domestic and creative lives. *Super Trouper* was in the end completed just weeks before its release, with the crucial title track being conceived and added at the last minute.

They had started work as early as January 1980, with the boys penning the first four or five songs in Barbados. While there, they met the celebrated British comic actor John Cleese, and discussed the possibility of him collaborating with them on a musical. The song "Happy New Year" was intended to play a vital part in this concept. Cleese pondered, then demurred, and once again the Bjorn/Benny musical was put on hold.

In March, Abba played two weeks of shows in Japan, and these turned out to be their last ever concerts outside Sweden. They would live with that: they had never been fond of life on the road (or, if they had, the novelty had long since worn off). The album's title track is a candid testament to their lack of enthusiasm for the rigours of touring. They carried on recording, though, and "The Winner Takes It All" emerged as a tragic and triumphant single, their first British chart-topper for two-and-a-half years. It made number one in over twenty countries, and its lyrics say much of Abba's state of mind and private preoccupations. Bjorn was drunk when he wrote the words. Agnetha cried when she finished singing them. She thinks it's the greatest ever Abba song. Many agree.

Peculiarly, the album title was decided on before the song of the same name existed. A "super trouper" is stagehand lingo for the huge spotlights used at big events like stadium shows or circuses. Just before deadline on the album, Bjorn and Benny were flushed with a rush of the old perfectionism, and decided that one more "killer" song was needed to make the album truly soar. The album title fit the new tune like a glove, and Frida sang another global chart-topper.

After years of abuse from snobbish critics, Abba were pleasantly surprised to receive some rare acclaim from music journalists for this album. *Melody Maker's* Lynden Barber declared, "Unlike some contemporaries, Abba make great pop songs that have magic – an ethereal quality that no critic can define, analyse or rationalise. 'The Winner Takes It All' is perhaps the supreme example of this ambience. 'Lay All Your Love On Me' and 'The Way Old Friends Do' are more than just songs – they're hymns." And *Record Mirror's* Mike Gardner had a point when he wrote; "The secret to Abba is never to hear them on an album, where the highs become a level. Each track needs to be savoured. Andersson and Ulvaeus are craftsmen whose ability to conjure up a memorable melody... shames most others." Reviews across the board were glowing. Benny and Bjorn smiled knowingly to themselves: it was too little too late, and they had never believed critics when it made more sense to believe their bank accounts instead.

In the UK, advance orders for the album – a million – broke all records. In its first day in the shops, it sold over 160,000 copies, rewriting the history books. Across the world, it was their fastest-selling album yet, shifting four million copies within two months. Abba even made healthy inroads into the American disco charts, and in 1981 were named Vocal Group Of The Year by the American Guild Of Variety Artists. In Britain they then released the first twelve-inch-only single to break the top ten. So this was Abba in decline?

Super Trouper

The final crossing of T's and dotting of I's on this track were completed just four weeks before the album's international release. Abba had cooled off on the track "Put On Your White Sombrero" at the last minute, and Benny and Bjorn swiftly wrote this replacement. Everyone in the camp was so taken by it that it became the second single, "The Winner Takes It All" having already re-established them at the top of the charts. As on much of the album, Benny's monolithic keyboard sound dominates, supported by heavy drums. Synths were to rule the Eighties, and Benny, for one, was quite happy with that turn of events.

"A 'SUPER TROUPER' IS STAGEHAND LINGO FOR THE HUGE SPOTLIGHTS USED AT BIG EVENTS LIKE STADIUM SHOWS OR CIRCUSES."

A huge hit (it goes without saying that it was insanely catchy), "Super Trouper" gave commercial momentum to the album that it might not otherwise have enjoyed: we'll never know. Its lyrical theme – of how little Abba enjoyed life on the road – seems incongruous at first for such a "positive" band. We're more used to heavy metal acts whining about the wine, women, drugs and travel. Abba bring their own distinct sensibility to it. From the phrase "I was sick and tired of everything, when I called you last night from Glasgow", this is strangely candid and confessional. It seems Benny can't help spilling his guts every time he picks up a pen now, and usually it's Agnetha's voice relating to and expressing his troubles and woes.

There are even glimmers of arrogance here, something we don't tend to associate with Abba…

as well as, of course, vulnerability. "Facing twenty thousand of your friends, how can anyone be so lonely? Part of a success that never ends, still I'm thinking about you only." There's both pride (at their fame) and hurt in there. Only Gene Pitney's "Backstage" has articulated the sadness of stardom more vividly.

The metaphor of the bright stage lights – the super troupers – is a tad tenuous, but Benny pulls it off. Interestingly, on the box of the original master tapes, the title's spelled differently, plumping for "Trooper". Photographer Lars Larsson's album cover further milked the notion, placing a harshly spotlit, all-but-deified Abba among a busy circus set-up, peopled by friends and associates. They'd wanted to shoot this scenario in London's Piccadilly Circus but local by-laws didn't allow, so Stockholm substituted.

Arguably the most "oom-pah-pah" of all Abba's major hits, "Super Trouper" transcends its plodding roots by means of its poignant lyrics and vocal. The a capella intro, as with "Take A Chance On Me", gives way to a thundering tempo. The backing vocals are as amazingly intricate as ever, and the middle eight has a heartstring-tugging, diva-ish quality before the key change kicks in after another acute a capella break. Bjorn and Benny's grunts of "soo-pah-pah troo-pah-pah" would be funny if they weren't so effective. And Benny's all-conquering, wibbly synths remind us that this was a hip and happening new decade where, for reasons perhaps best forgotten, synths were the *zeitgeist*.

Lyrically, this would have made a great parting shot for Abba but it's the not the only track here of which we can say that. "Super Trouper" was also their last ever British number one.

The Winner Takes It All

The release of "The Winner Takes It All", in July 1980, revitalised Abba's chart career, but again betrayed the very real heartache behind the scenes of the two shiny happy couples who dominated televisions and radios everywhere. Yes, they'd composed sad songs of hurtful relationships and break-ups before, but this seemed more intensely personal and soaked in genuine melancholia. Unlike the band's romances, which were cracking under the pressure of fame and a non-stop, excessive workload, the song has stood the test of time remarkably well.

1979 had been another frenetic and successful year for the group. They'd put on extravagant,

exhausting live shows. They'd embraced the disco era and, by doing so, conquered it. So, by 1980, even the notoriously prolific Bjorn and Benny were taking longer than usual to come up with songs for a new album. The group's internal relationships were suffering under the strain.

"The Winner Takes It All" was Bjorn committing his feelings about, and his reactions to, these experiences onto paper. Undoubtedly, it's among his greatest ever lyrics. The irony and pathos of Agnetha singing them (and many feel this is also her finest vocal performance) shouldn't be lost on any keen listener.

Abba songs were becoming, as often as not, more reflective, more poignant. Sure, they were still masters of the flippant, throwaway pop nugget, but a gentler, less gawdy sincerity increasingly crept into the songs' themes and motifs. "The Winner Takes It All" was the first of four U.K. smashes in quick succession that year, reaching number one for several weeks, and even making the top ten in the U.S. Their sentimental schlager roots had never fused with their pristine pop sensibilities so beautifully.

With its deceptively complex chord structure using repetition subtly, the song seduces the listener. "I don't want to talk about the things we've gone through," it begins. "Though it's hurting me, now it's history." There's a clumsy but affecting, almost accidental, grandeur to the lines "The Gods may throw a dice, their minds as cold as ice/And someone way down here loses someone dear." And if you're not moved by the tearful, humble climax of, "I apologise if it makes you feel bad/Seeing me so tense, no self-confidence", then you have a heart of granite. We may, even now, tend to think of Abba as karaoke pop puppets, but

songs such as this display their genius for tapping into the very best of pop: timeless, and yearning.

The skeleton of the song had come into being as a rough draft called "The Story Of My Life" – a faster, tighter concept. Bjorn tried some temporary lyrics, at one stage singing them himself in pidgin French in a vague attempt to evoke an Edith Piaf aura. But he and Benny sensed this melody merited something better. Bjorn took a demo tape of it home with him, and continued dabbling with it in private. One night he cracked open a bottle of whisky, drank it with impressive speed, got emotional, and wrote a complete lyric in under an hour. He's said it was the quickest lyric he ever wrote – and probably the best. He's added that writing while drunk never works – the result seems great at the time, but is invariably dreadful when you read it through the next day – except just this once. There were a lot of feelings about his divorce from Agnetha that he'd held inside for too long, and they came pouring out. Bjorn's also since stressed that the song isn't a literal description of his and Agnetha's romantic demise, but that real life "inspired" the story of a split-up.

For Agnetha's part, eighteen months on from the break-up she gave one of her greatest vocal interpretations while reportedly crying her eyes out. She's described it as the best of all Abba songs, where the lyrics are "deeply personal" and the music is "unsurpassed". To sing it, she had to act out a role: she couldn't let her real feelings take over and capsize the melody. But it wasn't long before she knew it was "a small masterpiece". Benny added that there are never any winners in a divorce.

Lasse Hallstrom's video, one of his most striking and memorable for Abba, fed the myth of Agnetha as the tragic, doomed, abandoned woman. The other three laugh and joke while she acts out the personification of moist-eyed melancholy. Most of the record-buying public believed the legend, conveniently forgetting that Bjorn had written the lyrics. Agnetha was dressed dowdily compared to her sex-kitten youth, and divorce was a hot theme of the times in Hollywood movies and leader articles. Abba had a new image, one where the mascara ran. And just as they'd been embraced by the masses as symbols of snug wedded bliss, they were now loved as resilient icons of emotional fallibility, sadness and suffering. Their fans wanted to comfort them (or at least Agnetha); to will them (or at least her) to survive adversity.

It was Abba, rather than their public, who were, not long after this latest pinnacle, to lose interest in Abba.

"ONE NIGHT HE CRACKED OPEN A BOTTLE OF WHISKY, DRANK IT WITH IMPRESSIVE SPEED, GOT EMOTIONAL, AND WROTE A COMPLETE LYRIC IN UNDER AN HOUR."

On And On And On

Usually described as a Beach Boys pastiche, "On And On And On", one of the earlier tracks to be recorded, is in fact nothing like the Beach Boys at all. A weird sonic hybrid of disco-throb and prescient New Romantic electro, it even pre-shadows the early Eighties textures of Duran Duran, Tears For Fears and Blancmange. The girls' vocals are treated, ending up kind of robotic and mechanical: German electro-pioneers Kraftwerk would have approved. Abba, with Benny getting into his synth shimmers and staccato piano stabs, sound every bit as "modern" as they wish to here, but still a touch aloof and sterile. You can envisage the crappy dancers on *Top Of The Pops* making

jerky "robotic" arm movements while daydreaming about crimping tongs and ra-ra skirts.

Again, the lyrics are striking, with further hints of boastful swaggering. It's all very un-Abba. Firstly, there's some ill-explained talk of "impending doom". Then, when a chap gets "kinda flirty" with our clockwork chanteuse, she takes advantage "of the fact that I'm a star/Shook my hair and took a casual stroll up to the bar/And as sure as hell this guy was coming up to me…" She knows how to blow him off, though: "I said I was not exactly waiting for the bus…" In truth, the bottom line on the addled lyrics to "On And On" is that they don't make sense, however long you peer at them. It's confirmation, though, that Björn's use of bad language has graduated from "heck" to "hell".

Frida
(Anni-Frid

Okay, so the chorus is a rip-off of the Beach Boys' 1968 hit "Do It Again", but outside of *that* reference, this is Abba trying to do futuristic. It's what one kindly describes as a "moderate" success. To confuse the issue even further, Mike Love – once a Beach Boy – covered the song for his solo album *Looking Back With Love* a year later.

> "ALSO A TOP TEN SINGLE IN AUSTRALIA, *ON AND ON AND ON* MADE NUMBER ONE ON THE US DISCO CHART, AS HAD *LAY ALL YOUR LOVE ON ME.*"

Perhaps he'd heard it in America. Also a top ten single in Australia, "On And On And On" made number one on the US disco chart, as had "Lay All Your Love On Me". Inspired by these "category" breakthroughs, Abba released the two songs as a double A-side twelve-inch-only single in the UK. The record reached number seven, which might seem moderate but was actually making history, being the first twelve-inch to make the top ten. Weren't Abba going to leave any space in the history books for anybody else?

Andante, Andante

After all that excitement and weirdness, it's almost a relief to find a run-of-the-mill, slightly bland ballad, written after the Barbados trip, complete with ooh-doesn't-that-guitar-sound-like-a-seagull "atmospheric" noises. Benny's piano and Bjorn's strumming guide a tender, gentle song: andante inferno, it isn't. When, for the chorus, what seem to be a million voices come in for several thousand different backing vocal lines, you're reminded that it's Abba. The track's warmth grows on you, and there's a cute false ending. The line "Tread lightly on my ground" is innocently reminiscent of W B Yeats' immortal caution, "Tread softly, for you tread on my dreams".

Me And I

Frida took Eartha Kitt as her inspiration for this quirky tale of the schizophrenia within us all. The increasingly confident Bjorn again lets his imagination roam free, promoting Frida into a cabaret vocal with elements of genuine darkness. "I am to myself what Jekyll must have been to Hyde", she purrs and snarls, while "cool" Eighties keyboards bubble beneath her, and faintly funky guitars underline her faux-angst. Benny's grand instrumental sections sound dated now, being the sort of keyboard bombast you only hear at opening ceremonies for Olympic Games. There's some techno-trickery on the voice, too, as Benny and Bjorn, in love with their new studio, play around with their gleaming Eighties tools. Generally they sacrifice some of Abba's distinctive sound through

doing that on this album, but overall it has a more cohesive, uniform feel than some of their more peripatetic offerings.

Surely this is the only Abba song to declare, "Sometimes I have toyed/With ideas that I got from dear old Dr. Freud". Respect! It's thus not quite as alarming as it might have been when Frida sharply concludes that "Everyone's a freak."

Happy New Year

If tracks like "Me And I" show how fascinating Abba could be when they let their dark, existential inner Swede take over from the perma-grin façade, "Happy New Year" - which Benny and Bjorn liked so much that they tried (and failed) to persuade John Cleese to help them write a whole musical around it – shows how dreary and flaccid their ballads could be when intended for "the stage". The concept had come to them on the plane to Barbados: they wanted to set a musical around a bunch of people, in a room on New Year's Eve, looking back on the past and forward to the future.

Yet this comes across as a befuddled lyric. Bjorn has been heard to refer to it as "political", which is fairly baffling. With its Broadway chorus, orchestral flourishes and general moping about "the dreams we had before… all dead, nothing more… than confetti on the floor", "Happy New Year" is bitter and cynical where "The Winner Takes It All" is sincere and moving. Perhaps Bjorn should have hit the whiskey again. Or hit Benny with the bottle.

As a statement on the beginning of the Eighties, it's fuzzy and forlorn: "In another ten years' time, who can say what we'll find?" Even the usually reliable Lasse Hallstrom's accompanying video was one of the director's most excessively obvious and depressing.

For reasons probably best known to Abba's accountants, "Happy New Year" sulked its way onto a 1992 double A-side release with "Thank You For The Music".

Our Last Summer

Recorded during the same spell of creativity as "The Winner Takes It All", this finds Frida singing the story of one of Bjorn's teenage romances, which took place in France. Again, Bjorn seems to be working through some long-repressed memories and attempting to ascertain who he is by re-evaluating his past. On the *Voulez-Vous* album, he had given the impression of a man

trying to lose himself in booze, parties and flings. Now, re-married, he's more ruminative, and with it more melancholy.

It's awkward though, that a woman is singing his words: they often end up falling between two stools. A song begins as a from-the-heart Bjorn confessional, then mutates clumsily into something expressed from a female perspective. "Our Last Summer" is a classic example. Bjorn is dreamily recalling his young affair by the Seine, "strolling down the Elysee". But the gender reversal scuppers him early on: "You talked of politics and philosophy, and I smiled like Mona Lisa", sings Frida. Which puts us in the position of assuming: well, Bjorn must have been talking about politics and philosophy to a vacuous airhead. Yet it's a sweet, gently funny song, which reiterates how far Abba (especially Bjorn) have moved on from those old happy-holiday ditties Stig used to insist upon…

> **"OUR LAST SUMMER IS A CLASSIC EXAMPLE. BJORN IS DREAMILY RECALLING HIS YOUNG AFFAIR BY THE SEINE, 'STROLLING DOWN THE ELYSEE'."**

In places, it almost echoes the Roxy Music classic "A Song For Europe" with its "classy" tourist references, then blows it by adding "Those crazy years – that was the time of flower power." Then comes the big twist, as Frida/Bjorn winces and admits: "And now you're working in a bank – the family man, a football fan/ And your name is Harry/How dull it seems…" The way Frida spits out the words "football fan", as if this makes Harry a child molester, is priceless. "Yet you're the hero of my dreams", she signs off, more kindly.

A great track, this, with its "fear of growing old and slowly dying" another indication of Bjorn's growing maturity and broodiness. Frida sings with greater resonance and tremolo than usual, and the guitar solo is really quite histrionic, untamed and rocky for Abba, who generally couldn't rock even when they tried to. (Even Michael Tretow confirmed this). The dummy guitar rush, as Frida lays into football fans and bank workers, is like 10cc at their most inventive.

The Piper

It is impossible to believe this was conceived in Barbados. *Super Trouper* is a cohesive album, except for these three-and-a-half minutes, which are about as entertaining as a tracheotomy. Abba lapse back into their cheesiest and most obsolete schlager tendencies for a god-awful dirge which defiled the b-side of the "Super Trouper" single.

Flute-based refrains, military-style drumming: this feels like it's about to break out into a mediaeval jig or claim to be at one with the elves and pixies or some such nonsense. It may think it's "folk".

Certainly it's unlistenable. And it's Eighties like Tiny Tim was Eighties. A strong contender for Abba's worst ever moment.

What is really bizarre is that the 1978 Stephen King novel *The Stand*, wherein the main character is a despotic, if seductive, leader of men, inspired the lyrics. This prompted Bjorn to claim the song was "political" and was about the threat of fascism, and his fear that it might rise again.

Of course, it's extremely well-documented that Abba never took drugs…

Lay All Your Love On Me

Underrated, and thought by many to be a sizeable influence on the early Eighties electro-pop movement (recently itself revived as "electroclash"), "Lay All Your Love On Me" has even been called "proto-techno". A hit in its own right, as mentioned earlier, its heavy wash of sequencer-driven synth chords throbs along to a Giorgio Moroder-esque, cold disco beat. Moroder did something quite similar to this on Sparks' "Beat The Clock". It was surely heard and admired by Human League, Soft Cell, Pet Shop Boys, Erasure and countless Eighties movers and shakers.

With a whopping great chorus, the song casts Agnetha – in fine voice again – as a woman afflicted by the green monster of jealousy. Possessive to a fault, this "grown woman" pleads to her lover, "don't go wasting your emotion". The song boasts a world-class scene-setting opening couplet: "I wasn't jealous before we met/ Now every woman I

see is a potential threat." Later, it rhymes "sensible" with "incomprehensible", which is in itself also pretty damn godlike.

This may be the last flicker of Abba's disco period, with a faint whiff of "Gimme! Gimme! Gimme!" (and, like that track, it's a huge favourite in gay pop culture). It has an odd melancholy grandeur too, though. It's almost like Agnetha is singing a hymn over a slutty backing track. And it's gorgeous.

The Way Old Friends Do

The show-stopping finale to their last tour, this unapologetic schmaltz involved the foursome linking arms front stage around Benny's accordion, pushing the audience's weepy buttons. A live recording from London's Wembley Arena in November 1979, the band considered it good enough to feature on a studio album. It may be a soppy rewrite of "Auld Lang Syne" but, in terms of sound, they were right. The vocals are astonishingly clear and pure and true for a live piece. If nothing else, it shows off the group's class and telepathic understanding as singers. And the big emotional punch may be as musically corny as can be, but it's undeniably there.

And with lines like, "Times of joy and times of sorrow/We will always see it through", this is another tune which would have made a great and very cinematic signing-off song for Abba. But they weren't ready to pack it all in just yet. They had one more album in them, and Bjorn and Benny were getting seriously interested in all those new, shiny, sexy, electronic Eighties gadgets…

BONUS TRACKS on 2001 Reissue:
Elaine

One of the first songs written for the album, but then relegated to the b-side of "The Winner Takes It All". It's a shame, as it's a fine example of all the worthwhile breakthroughs and tasteless excesses of the era. Synths chirrup away crazily and the beat is tub-thumpingly unsubtle. Some of the vocals are treated and phased (ooh, let's see what this switch does), and we're unnervingly reminded of Cliff Richard's "Wired For Sound" spell. But it rumbles along in its own eager-to-thrill way.

Poor old Elaine, however, has a rotten time, whoever she is. You wonder who Bjorn is writing about. Surely not Agnetha? Please? "Elaine" endures a miserable, frustrated existence, even if her name makes a catchy hook. She's "like a goldfish in a bowl", in a "dead end street". Oh dear, Benny really was growing up. Which is a good thing, right?

Put On Your White Sombrero

Dumped at the last minute for the title track (hurrah!), but rescued after fourteen years for inclusion on the *Thank You For The Music* box set (boo!). Sung by Frida like an over-strident school-ma'm with a janitor's broom up her jacksy, it's a baroque bash at a Tex-Mex take on "Fernando", complete with laboured use of castanets. Mangling a cowboy movie metaphor, it seems to be telling the bad guy to get on his horse. It's grim. It's not how the West was won. But thankfully, Abba weren't quite ready to ride off into the sunset just yet…

THE VISITORS 1981

THE VISITORS (CRACKIN' UP)

HEAD OVER HEELS

WHEN ALL IS SAID AND DONE

SOLDIERS

I LET THE MUSIC SPEAK

ONE OF US

TWO FOR THE PRICE OF ONE

SLIPPING THROUGH MY FINGERS

LIKE AN ANGEL (PASSING THROUGH MY ROOM)

Bonus tracks on reissue:

SHOULD I LAUGH OR CRY

THE DAY BEFORE YOU CAME

CASSANDRA

UNDER ATTACK

Recorded March 1981 - November 1981 at Polar, Stockholm.

Produced by Benny Andersson and Bjorn Ulvaeus. Engineered by Michael B. Tretow.

Musicians: Benny Andersson (keyboards, synths); Bjorn Ulvaeus (acoustic guitars); Lasse Wellander (electric and acoustic guitars); Janne Schaffer (guitars); Rutger Gunnarsson (bass); Ola Brunkert (drums); Per Lindvall (drums); Ake Sundqvist (percussion); Jan Kling (flute, clarinet); The Three Boys (mandolins on "One Of Us").

Vocals by Abba.

ABBA'S EIGHTH AND FINAL ALBUM WAS OFTEN A BLEAK, TROUBLED AND TROUBLING AFFAIR, ENLIGHTENED BY FLEETING FLASHES OF THE OLD MAGIC. IT'S AS FAR FROM THEIR POPTASTIC EARLY SOUND AS YOU COULD CONCEIVE. PEOPLE WHO LOVED ABBA "IRONICALLY" THINK IT'S A TORTURED WORK OF WRIST-SLASHING GENIUS. PEOPLE WHO LOVED ABBA WITHOUT KNOWING WHAT IRONY WAS — I.E. THE VAST MAJORITY OF THE WORLD'S POPULATION — JUST DIDN'T GET IT, AND SO ABBA'S GOLDEN AGE WAS ABOUT TO END.

Since Benny and Frida had divorced in early 1981, no time had been wasted in finding new partners. Benny was to marry television reporter Mona Norklit before the year was out, and Frida took up with a billionaire businessman, Bobo Hjert, in a "free relationship, free of demands". The papers and media continued to milk the two Abba couples' splits, inventing all manner of bizarre liaisons for them, but despite the pressure Abba still enjoyed making music together at Polar Studios. They didn't care what the headlines might say: for them it was quite straightforward – Agnetha and Frida loved singing, it was what they did. And Benny and Bjorn were still good pals and, after years of honing their telepathic

shorthand, weren't about to dissolve their song-writing partnership.

No, if Abba *were* to fade away shortly, it wouldn't be through any personal grievances. It was just that the musical format was getting a little stale for them. They wanted to branch out, try new things. But the studio, as they recorded *The Visitors*, was a reasonably amicable and laid-back place to be. The sessions may even have allowed the couples to find closure, to clearly separate their working rapport from their home lives.

Bjorn's lyrics became more frank and personal than ever, and "When All Is Said And Done" is obviously his testament to Benny and Frida's divorce. On the purely technical side, though, the recording proved problematic. Michael Tretow was encountering difficulties with some of Polar's new equipment, and *The Visitors* often sounds colder, less human, than Abba's previous body of work. Whether this was intentional or accidental, it makes for a more distressing, downbeat sign-off.

And yet for all the band members' maturity about working together, there's an alternative take on this period. Benny has recalled that the sessions were a slog, and Bjorn has given away that the atmosphere could – understandably – be chilly at times. He didn't like to ask either vocalist to try a line again, for fear they'd bite his head off. Frida has expressed it best, conceding that the joy had gone... and, therefore, the reason for being Abba. The group were all a bit tired of each other, and had grown apart. Undeniably, some sadness or bitterness seeped through into the music.

In a which-came-first-the-chicken-or-the-egg? situation, this is underlined by the fact that Frida and Agnetha don't sing together on the verses of any single song. Bjorn had initiated this, as his lyrics were getting increasingly idiosyncratic and real. He wanted solo interpretations. Benny wasn't keen on this development, and by the end of the sessions wasn't converted. His own decision to strip away the "wall of sound" tricks and let the emotions come through sparser arrangements was equally significant in making *The Visitors* such a frosty, and perhaps unfocussed, album.

"THE ENERGY HAD RUN OUT, BJORN LATER COMMENTED. 'THAT'S HOW IT FELT AT THE TIME.' BJORN AND BENNY WERE KEEN TO REACH FOR (AND CLOSE TO REALISING) THEIR NEXT DREAM: THEIR MUSICAL."

With songs about children leaving the nest, the passing of time, kinky love triangles and the perils faced by Soviet dissidents, *The Visitors* was never going to be *Ring, Ring*. "One Of Us" – a great lost-love song by anyone's standards – was a big hit, but not that big, only reaching number three in Britain. And the album topped the charts in quite a few countries, including the UK (where advance orders were around 700,000), but fewer countries than they had come to expect. "One Of Us" was Abba's last major hit. The loyal public's lukewarm response to the album confirmed the secret suspicions lurking inside each individual member: had Abba, as an idea, run its course? Should they step aside, and simply let the Eighties be the Eighties without them?

In the early part of 1982, both Bjorn and Benny had children with their new wives. Frida went to work with Phil Collins on her best-known solo album (her first for seven years), *Something's Going On*. Bjorn and Benny held talks with potential collaborator Tim Rice about their long-postponed musical, *Chess*. By May, Abba reconvened at Polar. They'd intended – after dabbling in these solo and extra-curricular projects – to record another album, but their famously prolific zeal was wavering. Their hearts clearly weren't in it.

Eventually, it was agreed that they'd release a compilation (double) album; *The Singles: The First Ten Years*. It would include just two brand new songs, which would be released as singles: "The Day Before You Came" (the last track they recorded), and "Under Attack" (the last they released). Witnesses have reported that there was a sense of closure in the air in the studio when these tracks were completed. All four Abba members made the right noises about the group's future, but evidently they all knew the end of an era loomed.

"The energy had run out," Bjorn later commented. "That's how it felt at the time." Bjorn and Benny were keen to reach for (and close to realising) their next dream: their musical. They'd been talking about this for nearly ten years and its time had come. The fact that the greatest hits album was a massive success while the singles stalled ("The Day Before You Came" peaked in the UK charts at a humiliating number 32 – unthinkable a year or two earlier for Abba) also told the band it was time to move on. By the end of 1982, they'd officially "taken a break"…

> "BJORN AND BENNY GOT THEIR HEADS DOWN WITH TIM RICE, AND BY 1986 *CHESS* WAS A POPULAR ALBUM AND STAGE SHOW."

Bjorn and Benny got their heads down with Tim Rice, and by 1986 *Chess* was a popular album and stage show. Both Frida and Agnetha made solo albums (Agnetha working with Blondie producer Mike Chapman and 10cc/Wings man Eric Stewart). Somehow, things moved on, and the "break" became permanent. None of them were particularly keen to revive the Abba team. For a brief while they hovered around the prospect of another album – *Opus 10* – but it didn't happen. Over the course of the Eighties, their remarkable legacy became as neglected and unhip as one of the most successful in pop history can be.

They had always been a little uncool and naff – now they were those things *without* the stunning sales figures. But as the Nineties swung around, and the 1992 release of *Abba Gold* shifted over twenty million copies, the CD generation excavated the legend. The songs won over a whole new audience (and rekindled the spark in the old one). To this day you can't leave the house without hearing "Dancing Queen" or "Knowing Me, Knowing You". The stage musical, *Mamma Mia*, gave Benny and Bjorn a fresh format in which to play with these songs, and Abba entered the twenty first century with their music as popular and ubiquitous as ever. An older, more reflective Agnetha and Frida have

mixed feelings about the time of their lives. Agnetha's tried to avoid fame like the plague. Benny and Bjorn have established a comfortable working relationship with their past. And the public at large? For them, it's still love…

The Visitors (Crackin' Up)

With its landscape of techno-lite swirls and synthesiser twinkles, "The Visitors" – note that ominous sub-title – is so very "early Eighties" that it's almost a parody The slightly disembodied vocals twist and warp (in a manner not entirely dissimilar to, say, This Mortal Coil's cover of "Song For The Siren"), and the atmosphere gathers and builds like dark clouds. There's a sense of high drama: you have to say that if Abba had been brave or reckless enough to keep this up through-out the whole album, it really would have been a classic of arty angst. They don't, and it isn't. But they did enough here to alienate large chunks of their mainstream audience, who saw the shadows and thought: I don't wanna go *there*.

When the song switches into the "crackin' up" refrain, it becomes more recognisably Abba. The tune rehashes "Summer Night City" with sharp staccato Eighties mannerisms. Thematically, its look at the dangerous existence of Soviet Union dissidents is less than specific. It hints at the fear of the unwanted knock on the door, and may be a vague snipe at Swedish political conformity. Bjorn was no Che Guevara, though he did occasionally moan about "the authorities". The song works better if you blithely assume the feelings of paranoia and

breakdown expressed are more of a personal statement by Bjorn concerning the states of mind of the now less-than-jolly characters in the band.

Others interpreted Bjorn's new-found obscurity as referring to some kind of body-snatching alien invaders. Or was it a summation of Abba's own soon-to-end journey to the centre of The Pop? Or were people reading too much into this because Abba weren't singing about banging a boomerang?

Head Over Heels

The second single from *The Visitors*, (after "One Of Us"), and one of Abba's most resounding British flops: this was their lowest-selling single since "I Do, I Do, I Do, I Do, I Do", seven years previously. Abba's unwillingness to put energy into promoting it didn't help matters. Neither did hiccups during production, later confessed by Michael Tretow, who was battling against the "too perfect" now digital tape recorder at Polar.

"IT WAS – LIKE, TO AN EXTENT, *ON AND ON* AND *MONEY, MONEY, MONEY* – ANOTHER TALE OF A GREEDY MATERIALIST."

It was – like, to an extent, "On And On" and "Money, Money, Money" – another tale of a greedy materialist. The woman in question is evidently well off: one wonders if Bjorn was writing about anything his audience could relate to here. He retains his sense of humour, though: "Her man is one I admire/He's so courageous but constantly tired/Each time when he speaks his mind/She pats his head and says, "That's all very fine"/Exert that will of your own… when you're alone."

Musically it's again very Eighties, the synths and rhythms bringing to mind such short-lived stars as Howard Jones, Nik Kershaw and the Thompson Twins. One look at the pastel jackets that Bjorn and Benny were wearing marks the era. There's also a faint hint of a waltz rhythm going on, and, this still being Abba, the chorus is strong. It wasn't the song that caused the record to flop, as such; it was the fact that people were into new bands, new sounds, new styles. And even Abba themselves were itching to explore some of those avenues.

When All Is Said And Done

Frida sings Bjorn's fine lyrics – probably about her break-up from Benny – over a Euro-rock burble which predicted some of her own solo material to come. The production here is undercooked (for once). If Benny's keyboards drown out any guitars, as usual, at least now he could say he was being "of the moment". This was to be the decade of keyboard wizardry. Did that make Benny ahead of his time?

Recorded in March 1981, many outside the US (where it performed respectably) thought this should have been a single. Bjorn allowed that it was "more or less" inspired by his friends' split. There were many overdubs, but Frida's vocal is one of her best, bristling with anger, sadness and regret. The words are both subtle – "both of us can feel the autumn chill" – and bold – "in our lives we have walked some strange and lonely treks/Slightly worn but dignified and not too old for sex". It's a testament to resilience, to human beings' ability to bounce back (eventually) from heartbreak, dust themselves off, and irrationally go searching for the mirage of true love all over again.

Soldiers

Don't worry – there's no military-style drumming. However, the rhythm is a tad leaden, and seems uncertain of what it's meant to do, or even what it *wants* to do. Dare we say, a bit like Abba at this stage? The guitar licks are quite tasty though. Very much one of Abba's more inconsequential numbers, "Soldiers" is "Fernando" without the fire, an anodyne fanfare for the common squaddie. It was possibly written around the same time as the title track, so could therefore be "political" by Bjorn's standards, while Agnetha enigmatically commented that it was about fear.

> "IT'S *THANK YOU FOR THE MUSIC* WITH A DEGREE, WHICH ISN'T NECESSARILY AN INSULT."

I Let The Music Speak

Abba certainly have let the music speak when it comes to this broad ballad: they've rarely passed judgement on it. It's evidently another example of Benny and Bjorn flexing their stage musical muscles, trying another run at what it would be like to write for the West End or Broadway. And in true "big musical" fashion, the lyrics are either clever or too clever. It's "Thank You For The Music" with a degree, which isn't necessarily an insult. It's also overlong and drawn-out, which is.

The backing vocals go all operatic, having evidently heard Queen pomp-ing up the likes of "Somebody To Love", and the flutes and clarinets towards the fade are chocolate-box sweet. In truth, *The Visitors* is the last Abba album you'd expect to find this track on...

One Of Us

A yearningly great song and, for many, the album's saving grace. Nobody did three minutes of lost-love better (except possibly The Carpenters, which this echoes). It even flourishes despite a misguided "reggae" arrangement. Yes, "One Of Us" survives a cod-ska arrangement that makes Bucks Fizz's "Land Of Make Believe" sound like Peter Tosh. It survives The Three Boys strumming their mandolins over the opening. It would have been much, much better as a sparse heartbreaker. Yet even so, the faultless melody and near faultless lyric carry it, as does Agnetha's nerve-shredding vocal. And when Frida piles in alongside her old friend/rival for the choruses, well, it's just like old times...

Recorded in the fall of 1981, it was the lead single and the band's last worldwide smash. Benny had harboured doubts about its worth, but Bjorn pushed for it (as, rightly, so did the record companies). It was number one in Holland, Belgium and West Germany, and number three in Britain. It couldn't do much about the territories which had lost interest.

The song's twist is worthy of Burt Bacharach collaborator Hal David. The narrator tells of how she felt trapped in a relationship, frustrated that she was being denied other, more exciting romances. So she left. Now "one of us" is lonely, feeling sorry for herself and waiting for a phone call from the man she jilted. It doesn't come.

Two For The Price Of One

Once again, it's striking how often Abba lurch from the sublime to the ridiculous. From the torchy "One Of Us", we screech into this silly Beatles pastiche, wherein Bjorn not only sings lead for the first time in ages but also brings out his inner wacky zany funny guy. Who, as we've learned in earlier chapters, sadly isn't all that funny.

Here he relates the story of a "trivial" cleaner who answers a lonely hearts ad, which promises "two for the price of one". He calls up (we hear the phone ringing), and an Alice Whiting picks up. She tells him that he's in for the time of his life with – here's the totally hilarious twist – her *and her mother*. What a scream!

Slipping Through My Fingers

As if to atone for that, Bjorn now gets serious for the rest of the album. "Slipping Through My Fingers" is a sweet but not-too-sugary song about the feelings of "melancholy and guilt" he had experienced a year earlier, as he'd waved his daughter Linda off to her first day at school. Like most parents, he sighs that her younger years seem to have flown by too quickly, and he hasn't given her all the joyful adventures he intended to. Agnetha – who else – sings with understanding and restrained passion. Bjorn and Agnetha by now shared a perfectly affable if more detached relationship, cemented by their love for Linda.

As a song about having to let go, "Slipping

Frida feature on the final version. Frida loved it, and it's a wonderful closer to Abba's "official" album career. A keyboard emulates a watch ticking, Frida sings as if enunciating a hymn, and for once the atmosphere is understated throughout. Haunting and elegaic, it makes you wish that Abba had exercised such beautiful and brave restraint more frequently. The album's sleeve designer based his imagery on it – hence the dark paintings of angels, the overbearing golden-brown light, and the sense that each member of Abba is isolated from the others. All of which added to the rumours – even before Abba knew it for sure – that this was the farewell album.

"In the twilight hour I am alone… in the gloom…" Bjorn's most forlorn lyrics yet are ambivalent and obscure, but firmly desolate. One close friend of the band has remembered him murmuring quietly at the time that, as a group, the four of them had given everything they had left to give.

Through My Fingers" bears extra resonance in the context of Abba's imminent demise. Agnetha has recalled that it felt very right and true to sing such a song, and that Bjorn had captured their mutual thoughts very appositely.

Like An Angel Passing Through My Room

Agnetha described this as Abba's most "naked" recording. In fact neither she nor Bjorn can be heard on it, as after several experiments the song was stripped right down – only Benny and

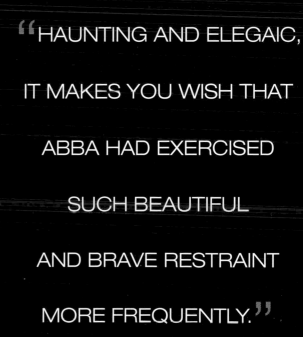

"HAUNTING AND ELEGAIC, IT MAKES YOU WISH THAT ABBA HAD EXERCISED SUCH BEAUTIFUL AND BRAVE RESTRAINT MORE FREQUENTLY."

just generic Eighties synth stuff, nothing special. It doesn't really go anywhere but into the "of its time" category. But that vitriolic lyric gets you playing the favourite Abba fan parlour game: who *did* Bjorn write it about?

The Day Before You Came

Although it's not one of their best-known numbers, this is a song which dedicated Abba-philes swear by. The last track ever recorded by the group, it managed the disastrously low chart placing of 32 in Britain but did less embarrassingly elsewhere, making the top five in some European countries. It also gave the loudest hint yet that Bjorn and Benny were itching to leave pop behind and move into musical theatre.

This can be seen in the archly detailed lyrics, reminiscent of the subtler work of such giants as Jimmy Webb and Hal David, which find a woman (Agnetha) listing all the run-of-the-mill, ordinary things she did the day before a lover came and rocked her world, turning black-and-white to colour. It's rich in wit and contrast; a far cry from, say, er, 1976's "Dum Dum Diddle". Benny is the sole musician featured.

In the song, the chanteuse reflects that she must have, she *supposes*, left her house at eight, caught the usual train, read the paper, got to her office desk, pushed some paper around, gone to lunch at "the usual place" with "the usual bunch"… you get the picture. Yet some of the dry insight here is on a par with an acclaimed indie seer like Morrissey. "I must have lit my seventh cigarette at half past

BONUS TRACKS on Reissue:

Should I Laugh Or Cry

The b-side of "One Of Us", which gives Frida an extraordinary lyric to deliver. Fundamentally, it consists of her slagging off her man for the duration of the song. He's "droning on in the usual way" and giving her "all his usual philosophy" and – even worse – his "trousers are too short". She has grown "cold as a stone". Musically, it's again two/And at the time I never even noticed I was blue…" She gets through her listless day – "A matter of routine, I've done it ever since I finished school" – and plods home. "I'm sure I had my dinner watching something on TV/There's not, I think, a single episode of *Dallas* that I didn't see/I must have gone to bed around a quarter after ten/ I need a lot of sleep, and so I like to be in bed by then."

As if all this wasn't wry and "un-Abba-ish" enough, the final verse glories in, "I must have read a while/The latest one by Marilyn French, or something in that style/It's funny, but I had no sense of living without aim/The day before you came." Philip Larkin, eat your heart out! (Indeed, more than one "hip, alternative" indie outfit – Blancmange, Jacques – has "ironically" covered this song, (usually to the bafflement of their blinkered fans).

Benny honed the original demo under the work-in-progress title of "Den Lidande Fageln". Translation? The suffering bird. For the video, Kjell Sundvall – who described the on-set atmosphere as very tense – replaced Lasse Hallstrom.

For all its ice-cool humour, the song *does*, with its sparse, stripped-down arrangement, evoke the hope and rapture of new love. There is a certain beauty to this being Abba's *bona fide* farewell. This is closure with class.

Cassandra

On the flipside of that under-trumpeted gem, you'll find this drab, umpteenth re-write of the themes of "Elaine", structured like "Fernando" but far less precisely or effectively. "Cassandra" is a song about a legendary prophetess of doom, whom everyone doubted, but who turned out to be visionary and correct. Wonder why she was on Bjorn's mind? Recorded in early August 1982.

> "FOR ALL ITS ICE-COOL HUMOUR, THE SONG DOES, WITH ITS SPARSE, STRIPPED-DOWN ARRANGEMENT, EVOKE THE HOPE AND RAPTURE OF NEW LOVE."

Under Attack

Chiming Eighties pop, full of studio trickery, and in itself a crisp, inventive pop song. A theme of a woman being stalked seems dodgy in retrospect, given Agnetha's later experiences, but Bjorn wasn't to know this. At any other stage in Abba's career, "Under Attack" would have been a gigantic single. At this stage, it bombed, even though they tried to look young and relevant by dressing up in grungy leathers for the video (which was drowned in dry ice by the new director, who wasn't as at ease with Abba as Hallstrom had been). The single sneaked into the top five in the loyal Belgium and Holland, but in Britain only just made the top thirty. Okay, that's better than "The Day Before You Came" did, but when you start talking up such lowly chart placings – for Abba, of all people – then you know the jig's up.

Abba, in their heart of hearts, knew it too. Just before Christmas 1982 they performed the song live from Stockholm, by satellite, for Noel Edmonds' BBC programme *The Late Late Breakfast Show*. It was the last time that the four ever made music together in public.

> "A THEME OF A WOMAN BEING STALKED SEEMS DODGY IN RETROSPECT, GIVEN AGNETHA'S LATER EXPERIENCES."

OUTRO

When All Is Said And Done…

By 1982, Stig Anderson was tired, less volatile, and admitting to the Swedish press that he drank too much. His role with Abba – formerly that of father figure, occasional muse, and Svengali – had drifted: now, it seemed, what he did was look after the money.

When he started to get even that side of things – his forte – wrong, cracks appeared in his relationship with the group. He began to make loud mission statements on their behalf that they didn't agree with. In July he announced a "gala" they were to perform in Stockholm as individual performers. They denied their involvement, Bjorn even adding that they disassociated themselves completely from this "stunt". Things spiralled downwards from here. By 1983 Benny was claiming that Stig (who, at least in his own head, had masterminded a decade of glorious success) had never represented Abba. In more ways than one, Abba's golden years were over.

Frida's solo album *Something's Going On* had been motivated by the passion she felt for erstwhile Genesis drummer Phil Collins' mega-successful *Face Value* album, particularly the single "In The Air Tonight". She insisted on working with Collins as producer: given the esteem with which he and most musicians held Benny and Bjorn as producers, he was honoured to accept the offer. The resulting album featured songs written by Collins, Giorgio Moroder and Bryan Ferry, among others. There was even an adaptation of a piece by Dorothy Parker, Frida's favourite writer. The Russ Ballard-penned title track was a minor international hit.

By 1984 Collins was too much in demand to resume the collaboration, so Frida made the *Shine* album with Steve Lillywhite, the man behind the big booming Eighties sound of acts like Simple Minds, Peter Gabriel and early U2. Songwriters here included Big Country's Stuart Adamson, Lillywhite's wife-to-be Kirsty McColl, and Frida herself. Benny and Bjorn even contributed a number, "Slowly". Solo success never really ballooned for Frida, though. There have been further, less heralded releases, but it wasn't exactly as if she needed the money. From the mid-Eighties onwards she's lived mostly in Switzerland and devoted much of her time to environmental issues, occasionally coming out of retirement to play benefits for this cause

Agnetha's first English language solo album was *Wrap Your Arms Around Me*, recorded in 1983. Her choice of producer was Mike Chapman, who together with Nicky Chinn had been behind the early Seventies singles of The Sweet, Mud and Suzi Quatro which had so thrilled the early, glam-loving Abba. Chapman was at the top of the tree now, having produced global giants for Blondie and The Knack, and he brought in British journeyman rockers Smokie to play on the album. Russ Ballard was a featured writer again, and Agnetha and Chapman

also composed material, but the songs weren't world-beaters. Chapman cunningly played up Agnetha's sex appeal on the title track, and "The Heat Is On" was a token hit. Eventually the album sold two million copies, and "Can't Shake Loose" broke the top five in America.

The Eyes Of A Woman album followed in '85, Agnetha having chosen Eric Stewart, of 10cc and Wings fame, as producer. Stewart, Agnetha, Justin Hayward and Randy Edelman were among the composers used. "I Won't Let You Go" and "One Way Love" were singles. But Agnetha, feeling she'd proved a post-Abba point, was weary of the music industry. She was one celebrity who, when saying she wanted to spend more time with her family, meant it. The Swedish media has however harried her ever since, forcing her to become for lengthy periods a Greta Garbo-like recluse.

After 1987's bluntly titled *I Stand Alone* album, Agnetha tried to hide from public view. She married a surgeon in 1990 then divorced him in '93. Daughter Linda is a grown-up who's moved out from home. Agnetha attempted to dispel some of the more outlandish rumours about herself with a 1997 autobiography, *As I Am*, but, evasive and enigmatic, it only served to fan the flames of her mystique. There are always rumours that she's going to make a musical comeback, and these have seemed more plausible since the millennium.

"CHAPMAN WAS AT THE TOP OF THE TREE NOW, HAVING PRODUCED GLOBAL GIANTS FOR BLONDIE AND THE KNACK, AND HE BROUGHT IN BRITISH JOURNEYMAN ROCKERS SMOKIE TO PLAY ON THE ALBUM."

Benny and Bjorn went on to play *Chess*. Their long-cherished musical project finally bore fruition, first as an album, then a stage show. With many of the regular Abba musicians, lyricist Tim Rice, and singers like Elaine Paige and Barbara Dickson, songs like "I Know Him So Well" and "One Night In Bangkok" became major hits. The double album emerged in late 1984, and after much hard work and refining, *Chess* opened in London's Prince Edward Theatre in May '86: Frida attended. British reviews were ecstatic, American ones harsh: *Chess* played for over four years in the UK, but only six months in New York.

The pair had a taste for musicals now. Bjorn and his new family made their home in Henley-on-Thames, Bjorn berating Swedish politicians for the rate of 80% income tax they required him to pay. He and Benny have since worked on Swedish musicals, solo records and pet projects, and carried out production for other bands and friends. Benny has also scored acclaimed arthouse movies such as *Songs From The Second Floor*.

By the early Nineties, Abba were cool again. Erasure took a covers EP to number one in Britain, U2 sang Abba's praises, and the *Abba Gold* compilation proved a huge seller – as did the inevitable *More Abba Gold*. They were cleverly marketed as virtuoso master craftsmen rather than slightly comical cartoon characters. The move stuck: they had respect. Although Steve Coogan has since single-handedly waged a war to reduce them to figures of ridicule…

All the albums have been reissued with bonus tracks. With Abba adamant that no future reunion was ever on the cards, "tribute" bands such as Bjorn Again and Abba Gold have cleaned up for years by impersonating the seminal Swedes. "Make the most of them", Benny said in 1999. "It's the closest you'll get to seeing Abba. Abba will never reform."

In fact as recently as 2000 they turned down an absurd amount of money to play a one-off reunion tour, chuckling that pop is a young person's game. And almost as if to confirm this view, countless young persons – teenybop stars – have covered their songs lately.

Stig Anderson died in 1997; all the old Abba members (except Agnetha, who was ill) attended his funeral, with Bjorn hailing him as their "mentor".

Of course, Bjorn and Benny are still raking it in from the *Mamma Mia!* musical. This light-hearted romp (similar in spirit to the Australian film *Muriel's Wedding*, which also hung its story around Abba classics) has wowed punters since its London premiere in April 1999, breaking various box office records. Simply envisaged as "a good night out", it has given Bjorn and Benny an involvement with the old Abba catalogue again, and as well as delivering the more obvious hits, has brought songs such as "Slipping Through My Fingers" and "Our Last

"FOR THE FOURSOME, FROM IMPOSSIBLY HAPPY COUPLES TO MULTI-MILLIONAIRE DIVORCEES."

Summer" into a higher profile. And if the men who penned the songs might seem to be grabbing all the glory, they're always the first to point out that without Agnetha and Frida the Abba story would simply never have happened.

It was a long strange trip from "Waterloo" to "The Day Before You Came", from "Ring, Ring" to "Like An Angel Passing Through My Room". In the case of Benny and Bjorn, from bad clothes and beards and accordions to, well, bad clothes and beards and accordions. For Agnetha and Frida, from confident sex symbols to jittery, mysterious divas who shun photographers. For the foursome, from impossibly happy couples to multi-millionaire divorcees. But say the word Abba and people around the world, of all generations, think instantly of fun and frolics, of ebullient pop music that lifts your heart to the chandeliers, then, with a swoop of one of those melodramatic ballads, leaves it swinging there. Rarely in the field of artistic endeavour have four people worked so hard so the rest of us could hedonistically enjoy our playtime.

Leave 'em burning and then you're…
GONE.

CHRONOLOGY

1945

April: Bjorn Ulvaeus is born in Gothenburg on April.
November: Anni-Frid Lyngstad is born in Norway.

1946

December: Benny Andersson is born in
Vallinby, Stockholm.

1950

April: Agnetha Faltskog in born in Jonkoping.

1964

The Hep Stars' first single with Benny,
"A Tribute To Buddy Holly", released.
The Hootenanny Singers' first single with Bjorn,
"Jag Vantar Vid Min Milla", released.

1967

Frida's first single, "En Ledig Dag", released.

1968

Agnetha Faltskog's first (self-titled) album released.
Bjorn's first solo single, "Raring", released.

1969

Nightclub singer Frida meets Hep Star Benny for
the first time, in Malmo. By the end of the year
they are engaged. Bjorn and Agnetha meet for the
first time at a Stockholm television studio, and
start dating. The Hep Stars and The Hootenanny
Singers both split.

1970

First Benny & Bjorn single, "My Kind Of Girl",
and album, *Lycka*, released.

1971

Bjorn and Agnetha marry in July.

1972

Bjorn, Benny, Agnetha and Anni-Frid release the singles "People Need Love" and "He Is Your Brother".

1973

The quartet release the singles "Love Isn't Easy" and "Ring, Ring". The latter fails to win them a place in Eurovision, although both it and the album of the same name top the Swedish charts.

1974

The year of "Waterloo" and those costumes. Abba unforgettably win Eurovision in Brighton, England, and become overnight international sensations. They go to number one in the UK. A follow-up hit, however, proves elusive, as "Honey Honey" and "So Long" flop.

1975

Although another flop, "I Do, I Do, I Do, I Do, I Do", threatens to sink their career, Abba rediscover the winning formula with "S.O.S." and "Mamma Mia". The album *Abba* is bought by one in every twenty Swedes. Inexplicably, it sells lorry loads in eastern Europe and Australia, where "Mamma Mia" remains the biggest selling single in history. Even in America, "S.O.S." sells a million, and Abba appear on *Saturday Night Live* with Paul Simon.

1976

"Mamma Mia" is number one in the UK. Benny bemoans their Eurovision image, claiming they "just happened" to be in the contest, and he'd rather the band were perceived as the new Mamas and the Papas. This is their year: in Australia, Abbamania runs riot. "Fernando" and the peerless "Dancing Queen" give them further chart-toppers in Britain and many other countries. *The Greatest Hits* compilation and the *Arrival* album are gigantic successes.

In June, Abba perform at the Swedish Royal Wedding gala. They premiere "Dancing Queen", so everyone assumes it is written for the blushing bride. It isn't, but it gives them their first American number one. "Money Money Money" is another hit. A rumour that all four band members have been killed in a plane crash in Germany is quickly scotched.

1977

Abba's first world tour takes in 28 dates across Europe and Australia, including two nights at the Royal Albert Hall and two in front of crowds of twenty thousand in Adelaide. A Swedish journalist is the first to ask Agnetha if she has "the sexiest bottom in show business". "I don't know", she replies, "I haven't seen it."

Lasse Hallstrom (nowadays a major Hollywood

movie director) begins shooting *Abba – The Movie*. "Knowing Me, Knowing You" is another worldwide hit, reaching number one in Britain. Abba take six months "off" to write and record, and re-emerge with "The Name Of The Game" and "Take A Chance On Me", from the imaginatively-titled album *The Album*.

Abba buy an old cinema in Stockholm and begin converting it into their own Polar Studios.

1978

The band announce that there will be no tours or live dates this year. *Abba – The Movie* is released; Agnetha focuses on motherhood. In September they enter the disco wars, releasing "Summer Night City", a single despised by critics. Benny

and Frida, after nine years living together, marry in October, at their local church in Lidingo. The band appear on the Christmas editions of UK TV shows *The Mike Yarwood Show* and *Jim'll Fix It*, in the latter Jimmy Saville fixing it for two of their fans to meet them. Fifty thousand had written to apply.

1979

Agnetha and Bjorn stun their fans and the world's media by announcing their divorce. They will, however, continue to work together. And how: the band enjoy a relentless stream of hits as they embrace disco but still turn out anthemic ballads. The year's hits include "Chiquitita", "Voulez-Vous", "Does Your Mother Know", "Gimme! Gimme! Gimme! (A Man After Midnight)" and "I Have A Dream". *Greatest Hits Volume Two* and *Voulez-Vous* dominate the album charts. In September, Abba begin a marathon tour of North America and Europe, forty concerts in ten countries, which runs through to late November.

1980

The new decade begins with a specially-recorded Spanish-language album, *Gracias Por La Musica*. In March, Abba tour Japan, playing to over 100,000 rabid fans. It's to be their last major tour. "The Winner Takes It All" is another worldwide number one, and sees the band finally gaining some critical approval from cynical reviewers. The album and single *Super Trouper* reaches advance orders in the U.K. alone of a record-breaking one million, and eventually goes on to sell seven million internationally within a few weeks. Abba are forced to cancel a planned promotional trip to England, Germany and France after receiving letters threatening the lives of their children.

1981

Bjorn remarries in January. Benny and Frida announce divorce proceedings in February. Like Bjorn and Agnetha, they say they're happy to carry on working together. Bjorn's lyrics increasingly reflect the reality behind Abba's too-happy-to-be-true façade. The eighth and final Abba album, *The Visitors*, includes their last sizeable hit, "One Of Us". The album is another British chart-topper, but Abba are beginning to pull in different directions, creatively and personally.

1982

Despite recording some fascinating tracks like "The Day Before You Came" for the compilation *The Singles: The First Ten Years*, Abba's domination of the commercial arena is waning. Benny and Bjorn are more interested in pursuing their dreams of writing a stage musical, and for Agnetha and Frida there is little left to prove within the band framework. Abba decide to take "a break", which turns out to be their bitter-sweet end. Benny and Bjorn begin work on *Chess* with Tim Rice. Frida releases the *Something's Going On* album, produced by Phil Collins.

1983

Agnetha releases the *Wrap Your Arms Around Me* album, produced by Mike Chapman.

1984

Frida's album *Shine*, produced by Steve Lillywhite, is released.

1985

Agnetha releases her album *Eyes Of A Woman*, produced by Eric Stewart.

1986

Chess premieres in London.
Abba Live album is released.

1987

I Stand Alone, Agnetha's last recording to date, is released.

1992

Abba Gold introduces the band's music to a new generation and is a runaway hit.

1993

More Abba Gold, and a glut of tribute bands, fuel the revival.

1999

Mamma Mia, the musical based around Abba songs, premieres in London.

2001

Abba's eight studio albums are remastered and reissued with bonus tracks.

SELECTIVE DISCOGRAPHY

This discography is not definitive: a mere detailing of the many Abba compilation albums of the last two decades might approach telephone directory size. For this information, we respectfully suggest you consult your nearest record store, or an exhaustive website such as www.abbafiles.com. For track listings on the band's original studio albums, please see the start of the appropriate chapter. We have, however, sought to reflect the fact that Abba were possibly the ultimate singles band by listing every single release, plus B-sides, from their halcyon days… and beyond.

RECORDINGS AS ABBA:

Albums

1973 RING RING

1974 WATERLOO

1975 ABBA

1975 GREATEST HITS

1976 ARRIVAL

1977 THE ALBUM

1979 VOULEZ-VOUS

1979 GREATEST HITS VOL. TWO

1980 GRACIAS POR LA MUSICA

1980 SUPER TROUPER

1981 THE VISITORS

1982 THE SINGLES: THE FIRST TEN YEARS

1986 ABBA LIVE

1992 ABBA GOLD

1993 MORE ABBA GOLD

Singles

1972 PEOPLE NEED LOVE/ MERRY-GO-ROUND

1972 HE IS YOUR BROTHER/ SANTA ROSA

1973 LOVE ISN'T EASY/ I AM JUST A GIRL

1973 RING, RING (SWEDISH)/ AH VILKA TIDER

1973 RING, RING/ MERRY-GO-ROUND

1974 WATERLOO (SWEDISH)/ HONEY HONEY (SWEDISH)

1974 WATERLOO/ WATCH OUT

1974 HONEY HONEY/ KING KONG SONG

1974 SO LONG/ I'VE BEEN WAITING FOR YOU

1975 I DO, I DO, I DO, I DO, I DO/ ROCK ME

1975 SOS/ MAN IN THE MIDDLE

1975 MAMMA MIA/ INTERMEZZO NO. 1

1976 FERNANDO/ HEY, HEY, HELEN

1976 DANCING QUEEN/ THAT'S ME

1976 MONEY, MONEY, MONEY/ CRAZY WORLD

1977 KNOWING ME, KNOWING YOU/ HAPPY HAWAII

1977 THE NAME OF THE GAME/ I WONDER (DEPARTURE) (LIVE)

1977 TAKE A CHANCE ON ME/ I'M A MARIONETTE

1977 THANK YOU FOR THE MUSIC/ EAGLE (LIMITED RELEASE)

1978 SUMMER NIGHT CITY/ MEDLEY:
PICK A BALE OF COTTON

1979 CHIQUITITA/ LOVELIGHT

1979 VOULEZ-VOUS/ ANGEL EYES

1979 DOES YOUR MOTHER KNOW/ KISSES OF FIRE

1979 VOULEZ-VOUS/ DOES YOUR MOTHER KNOW
(12" ONLY)

1979 GIMME! GIMME! GIMME! (A MAN AFTER
MIDNIGHT)/ THE KING HAS LOST HIS CROWN

1979 I HAVE A DREAM/ TAKE A CHANCE ON ME (LIVE)

1980 THE WINNER TAKES IT ALL/ ELAINE

1980 SUPER TROUPER/ THE PIPER

1981 LAY ALL YOUR LOVE ON ME/ ON AND ON AND ON
(12" ONLY)

1981 ONE OF US/ SHOULD I LAUGH OR CRY

1982 HEAD OVER HEELS/ THE VISITORS

1982 THE DAY BEFORE YOU CAME/ CASSANDRA

1982 UNDER ATTACK/ YOU OWE ME ONE

1983 THANK YOU FOR THE MUSIC/ OUR
LAST SUMMER (LIMITED RELEASE)

1992 DANCING QUEEN/ LAY ALL YOUR LOVE ON ME
(E.P.)

1992 VOULEZ-VOUS/ SUMMER NIGHT CITY (E.P.)

1992 THANK YOU FOR THE MUSIC/ HAPPY NEW YEAR
(E.P.)

SOLO MATERIAL

BJORN ULVAEUS
Albums

1970 LYCKA (with Benny Andersson)

1982 CHESS (with Benny Andersson & Tim Rice)

1988 CHESS (Broadway Cast Recording)

*(also sixteen albums with The Hootenanny Singers,
chiefly throughout the Sixties).*

BENNY ANDERSSON
Albums

1970 LYCKA (with Bjorn Ulvaeus)

1982 CHESS (with Bjorn Ulvaeus & Tim Rice)

1987 KLINGA MINA KLOCKER

1988 CHESS (Broadway Cast Recording)

*(also ten albums with The Hep Stars,
chiefly throughout the Sixties).*

AGNETHA FALTSKOG
Albums

1968 AGNETHA FALTSKOG

1969 AGNETHA FALTSKOG VOL. TWO

1970 SOM JAG AR

1971 NAR EN VACKAR BLIR EN SANG

1973 BASTA

1974 AGNETHA

1975 ELVA KVINNOR I ETT HUS

1979 TIO AR MED AGNETHA

1980 NU TANDAS TUSEN JULELJUS
(with daughter Linda)

1983 WRAP YOUR ARMS AROUND ME

1985 EYES OF A WOMAN

1986 SJUNG DENNA SANG

1987 KOM FOLJ MED I VAR KARUSELL
(with son Christian)

1987 I STAND ALONE

ANNI-FRID "FRIDA" LYNGSTAD
Albums

1971 FRIDA

1972 MIN EGEN STAD

1976 FRIDA ENSAM

1982 SOMETHING'S GOING ON

1984 SHINE

1991 PA EGEN HAND

SOURCES

*Bright Lights Dark Shadows: The
Real Story Of Abba*
Carl Magnus Palm (Omnibus).

Abba: The Music Still Goes On
Paul Snaith
(Castle Communications).

Abba: The Name Of The Game
Andrew Oldham, Tony Calder and
Colin Irwin (Sidgwick & Jackson).

From Abba to Mamma Mia! Anders
Hanser & Carl Magnus Palm (Virgin).

Plus album sleeve notes to 2001
Universal/Polydor reissue series, by
Carl Magnus Palm.

INDEX